3/97

VERSITY OF
OLVER

☑ KT-384-816

Whisper of the Mother

Daughter and mother by Maureen Fitzgerald, Pohnpei, 1999.

Whisper of the Mother

From Menarche to Menopause Among Women in Pohnpei

MAUREEN H. FITZGERALD
*in collaboration with Eugenia Samuel
and Linda Phillip*

Foreword by
Mac Marshall

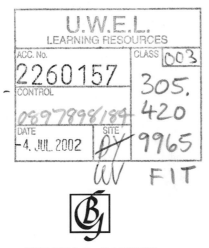

U.W.E.L.
LEARNING RESOURCES

ACC. No.
2260157

CONTROL
0897898184

DATE
-4. JUL. 2002

CLASS 003
305.
420
9965

SITE

FIT

BERGIN & GARVEY
Westport, Connecticut • London

Library of Congress Cataloging-in-Publication Data

Fitzgerald, Maureen H. (Maureen Helen)
    Whisper of the mother : from menarche to menopause among women in Pohnpei /
Maureen H. Fitzgerald ; in collaboration with Eugenia Samuel and Linda Phillip ;
foreword by Mac Marshall.
        p.   cm.
    Includes bibliographical references and index.
    ISBN 0–89789–818–4 (alk. paper)
    1. Women—Micronesia (Federated States)—Pohnpei.   2. Menstrual cycle—Social
aspects—Micronesia (Federated States)—Pohnpei.   3. Birth customs—Micronesia
(Federated States)—Pohnpei.   4. Pohnpei (Micronesia)—Social life and customs.
5. Social change—Micronesia (Federated States)—Pohnpei.   I. Samuel, Eugenia.
II. Phillip, Linda. III. Title.
GN671.C3F57   2001
305.4′09965—dc21   2001025703

British Library Cataloguing in Publication Data is available.

Copyright © 2001 by Maureen H. Fitzgerald

All rights reserved. No portion of this book may be
reproduced, by any process or technique, without the
express written consent of the publisher.

Library of Congress Catalog Card Number: 2001025703
ISBN: 0–89789–818–4

First published in 2001

Bergin & Garvey, 88 Post Road West, Westport, CT 06881
An imprint of Greenwood Publishing Group, Inc.
www.greenwood.com

Printed in the United States of America

⊗™

The paper used in this book complies with the
Permanent Paper Standard issued by the National
Information Standards Organization (Z39.48–1984).

10 9 8 7 6 5 4 3 2 1

Copyright Acknowledgments

The author and publisher gratefully acknowledge permission for use of the following material:

Excerpts from Gene Ashby, *A Guide to Pohnpei: An Island Argosy*. Kolonia, Pohnpei:
Rainy Day Press, 1983.

Excerpts from Gene Ashby, *Some Things of Value: Micronesian Customs as Seen by
Micronesians*. 2nd Ed. Kolonia, Pohnpei: Rainy Day Press, 1983.

Reprinted by permission of Waveland Press, Inc. from M.C. Ward, *Nest in the Wind:
Adventures in Anthropology on a Tropical Island* (Prospect Heights, IL: Waveland Press,
Inc., 1989). All rights reserved.

To the women of Pohnpei, to my sister-in-law, Barb, and to the mother who first whispered to me, my mother, Jerry, whose whispers I still hear today

Contents

Illustrations

Foreword

Mac Marshall

In a very thorough review of the post–World War II literature on medical anthropology for Micronesia, Rubinstein concludes that "medical anthropology itself has covered little ground and has garnered little attention from health care providers in the islands" (1999, p. 355). Fitzgerald's welcome volume represents one small step toward remedying both of these deficiencies, and it has several other virtues as well.

Perhaps its most significant contribution is that it is the first maternal-child health (MCH) study in Micronesia to use a life cycle approach to women's reproductive health (reflected in the subtitle: "from menarche to menopause"). In keeping with this, the women who were interviewed for the volume discuss their lives as marked by the biological processes of menstruation, pregnancy and birthing, postpartum motherhood, and menopause. Fitzgerald already has made significant contributions to these topics in her doctoral research with Samoans and related publications, and thus she is eminently well qualified to carry out the study summarized in this slender volume. The sections on pregnancy and birthing and postpartum motherhood together constitute nearly half the text, so despite the subtitle this is not really a book that focuses on menarche and menopause per se.

A second important contribution of this work is its collaborative nature. Fitzgerald worked closely with and relied heavily upon the language skills and cultural knowledge of Eugenia Samuel and Linda Phillip, and this teamwork clearly contributed to the quality and quantity of data they were able to gather in a short fieldwork period of two months. Such collaborative work is to be both applauded and encouraged in future medical anthropological studies in Micronesia.

The Federated States of Micronesia (FSM), like most of the rest of the Pacific, has become increasingly "urbanized," or town-oriented, and its urban areas typically include substantial ethnic and linguistic diversity. Pohnpei, as the FSM capital, reflects this diversity, and Fitzgerald's study captures this in the women interviewed. Well over half of the two dozen women interviewed were ethnically Pohnpeian, and the others included Mortlockese, Chuukese, and women from Palau, Mwoakilloa (Mokil), and Sapwuahfik (Ngatik). Although many aspects of MCH apparently are common across these different ethnic groups, we can hope for future longer-term and more in-depth follow-up research that might explore some of the anticipated cultural differences as well. For example, Ann Fischer's (1957) dissertation, Frances Caughey's (1971) master's thesis, and Leslie and Mac Marshall's (1979, 1980) articles on MCH in Chuuk offer a good basis for cross-cultural comparison between Pohnpei and Chuuk.

In sum, this exploratory study takes some desirable first steps toward developing a richer literature on MCH in Micronesia. As future work unfolds on this topic in the islands it will be important to position it within the wider medical anthropology literature that has accumulated on menstruation, menopause, birthing, and infant care and feeding (e.g., Beyene, 1986; Jordan, 1978; Lock, 1993; L. Marshall, 1985). In this way, knowledge from and about Micronesia will add to our wider understandings of these universal human processes, and information gathered elsewhere may contribute to the development of policies and programs in the FSM.

REFERENCES CITED

Beyene, Yewoubdar (1986). Cultural significance and physiological manifestations of menopause: A biocultural analysis. *Culture, Medicine and Psychiatry, 10,* 47–71.

Caughey, Frances B. (1971). Pregnancy and childbirth on Uman, Truk. M.A. Thesis, University of Pennsylvania.

Fischer, Ann (1957). The role of the Trukese mother and its effect on child training. Ph.D. Diss. Radcliffe College.

Jordan, Brigitte (1978). *Birth in four cultures: A cross-cultural investigation of childbirth in Yucatan, Holland, Sweden and Montreal.* St. Albans, VT: Eden Press Women's Publications.

Lock, Margaret M. (1993). *Encounters with aging: Mythologies of menstruation in Japan and North America.* Berkeley: University of California Press.

Marshall, Leslie B. (Ed.) (1985). *Infant care and feeding in the South Pacific.* New York: Gordon and Breach Science Publishers.

Marshall, Leslie B., & Marshall, Mac (1979). Breasts, bottles and babies: Historical changes in infant feeding practices in a Micronesian village. *Ecology of Food and Nutrition, 8* (4), 241–249.

——— (1980). Infant feeding and infant illness in a Micronesian village. *Social Science & Medicine, 14B,* 33–38.

Rubinstein, Donald H. (1999). Staking ground: Medical anthropology, health, and medical services in Micronesia. In Robert C. Kiste & Mac Marshall (Eds.), *American anthropology in Micronesia: An assessment* (pp. 327–359). Honolulu: University of Hawaii Press.

Preface

Despite the considerable attention directed toward maternal and child health in The Federated States of Micronesia (FSM) and elsewhere, there is very little recorded information about traditional beliefs, practices, and experiences associated with women's reproductive lives, the changes that have occurred, and the context they provide for understanding contemporary experiences. Because some of the key indicators of the health of a population, including FSM, are related to women and their health (e.g., birthrate, fertility rate, and maternal and infant mortality), a better understanding of this area from the women's perspective should help us better understand these often decontextualized statistics.

In addition, this information can contribute to actions designed to improve women's lives. For example, information on traditional birth related beliefs, practices, and experiences can be used to understand women's behavior in modern birthing contexts, and they can be used to design birthing environments that meet women's social, psychological, physical, and cultural needs—and still address the needs of the medical system and its personnel. Information on changes in the menstrual and birthing experience can be used to understand both the causes and consequences of culture change on women's lives and on their communities.

One of the purposes of this study was to explore some of these beliefs, practices, and experiences, to record them for posterity, and to use them to understand some contemporary issues, such as concerns about teenage pregnancies, the changing nature and role of families in contemporary life, and the potential for an increase in mental health concerns among young mothers. This study was designed as an exploratory study to determine whether there was a need for, or any community interest in, expanding the study, namely whether it would address issues of local concern. In addition, as local concerns were revealed, the research was modified to begin to address them.

This book is an adaptation of a report written in 2000 (Fitzgerald, 2000a). It is based primarily on research conducted on Pohnpei, FSM, from mid-April to mid-June 1999, although it builds on previous work conducted among Samoans (Fitzgerald, 1989; Fitzgerald, 1990; Fitzgerald, 1992) and nine years of short periods of work in Micronesia. It is based on several kinds of data: formal and informal interviews, casual conversations, observations of and participation in everyday activities and events, and readings of the literature. The formal and informal interviews were "key informant" interviews. Key informants included women, almost all of whom were mothers, at a various stages in their reproductive lives; female and male representatives of various local governmental and non-governmental organizations; and doctors and other health personnel. Some women spoke as key informants from more than one perspective, for example, as a woman who has given birth and as a doctor.

Most formal interviews (meetings specifically scheduled for the expressed purpose of talking about women's health issues) were tape-recorded with the permission of everyone present. If an interview was not audio recorded, generally because a tape recorder was not available, then extensive interview notes were produced shortly after the interview. Recorded English language interviews were transcribed verbatim. Interviews in other languages were transcribed as "summary translations." Summary translations have been used for several reasons. First, given the nature of the languages and the topic of the interviews, verbatim transcription would have contributed little at this point. Second, I wanted fuller summaries so I could prepare this report in the most timely fashion. The summarizing transcription process also allowed us to identify areas we needed to explore more fully in future interviews. All but two of the interview tapes were transcribed during the data collection period.

All the quotes in this text are in English, and are taken either directly from the tape recording or from a summary transcription of the tape. Some quotes have been edited into standard English, but an attempt has been made not to lose the spirit of Micronesian English. I will leave the task of presenting this information in the original languages to someone proficient in these languages. For now, the information is presented in a language that makes the information reasonably accessible to literate Micronesians and non-Micronesians.

Much of this book is based on data collected during 14 formal group and individual interviews with 24 women who ranged in age from 20 to 72 years. These women are from Pohnpei; Chuuk, including the Mortlocks; Mokil; Pingelap; and Sapwuahfik. Several of the women identify with more than one Micronesian group either because they have mixed parentage or because they have lived on Pohnpei for all or most of their life. At this stage in the project the focus was on Micronesians for two reasons: first, they represent the largest portion of the population of Pohnpei, and second, there is little published information on this topic for Micronesians.

The formal interviews generally lasted two to three hours. The shortest interview was with one of the 20-year-olds; it lasted 45 minutes. The longest interview was roughly five hours over two sessions. About halfway through the second session with this woman, another woman joined the session. Participation in the open-ended, ethnographic-style interviews was voluntary. Participants were interviewed in their language of choice with the assistance of one or two trained native language research collaborators. Participants were recruited through contacts in the community. The focus was on working with key informants who, by the nature of their lived experiences and/or because of their position in the community, could speak knowledgably on the topics.

An intense review of the literature, making particular use of the Micronesian Seminar library, supports the observation that little has been written on this topic in terms of Pohnpei. The most detailed information is found in the works by Martha Ward (1989) and Roger Ward (1977). The works by Ashby (1983a, 1983b), Demory (1976), Kihleng (1996), and a translation of a paper from the Japanese period by Yasuo (1940) offer some additional information. There is one work for Chuuk (formerly Truk) that is also very informative. This paper by Ann Fischer (1963), who, with her husband, John Fischer, also worked on Pohnpei, covers many of the same topics as in this book. Beyond these works there are "bits and pieces" and "in passing" comments in a variety of other works on Pohnpei. For the most part, the information acquired during the interviews and that in the written record, including that by Fischer, are consistent and complementary.

The research was supported in part by the University of Sydney (Dr. Fitzgerald's period of study leave and some travel funds) and the Micronesian Seminar (Pohnpei, FSM), directed by Father Francis X. Hezel, which provided a Pohnpeian home for the project and unlimited access to its facilities. The Department of Anthropology at the University of Hawaii at Manoa provided office accommodation for the period of study leave spent in Honolulu. Some of the information on menstruation (Fitzgerald, 2000b) was presented in a special session on menstruation at the Annual Meeting of the American Anthropological Association organized by Janet Haskins and Lene Pedersen. The opportunity to present was supported by a University of Sydney Overseas Conference and Travel Grant.

I would like to thank Eugenia Samuel and Linda Phillip for their incredible support and assistance. As a research team we would like to express our appreciation to the many people who contributed to this project through various kinds of support. This includes many people in Pohnpei, including staff in the Pohnpei Department of Health and the FSM Ministry of Health. We would like to say *kalahngan en komwi* to everyone, particularly the women who participated in the interviews, for sharing their time and knowledge with us.

Chapter 1

Introduction

In the old days, so women tell us, women learned about women's things, such as menstruation, pregnancy, birthing, and menopause, through the "whisper of the mother." There were no sex education classes in schools or open, public discussions with other women. In the past, women learned through personal experience and observation. They learned through listening to the stories their mothers and grandmothers told them in the evenings. They learned through soft, quiet, intimate talks with their mothers or by overhearing whisperings between women of their mothers' generation.

For most women, the whisperings about menstruation (*soumwahu en lih*) were not heard until after the fact, after they had their first menses. But there were also many women in the past who never heard any of the whisperings. Their mothers were too old or were otherwise unavailable. "Everything happened to her became a lesson after she already went through or experienced it, without prior advice from her mother."[1] Many young women today are like these women. As modern women of modern women they have not heard the whisperings or have not listened and remembered. Many women, even many in their 40s, do not remember the old beliefs or the reasons for some of the practices they and their mothers engaged in when they were pregnant and gave birth. They have intentionally, and unintentionally, exchanged many of the old ways, the old knowledge, for the new, the modern, and the Western.

Because so much of women's knowledge in Pohnpei was shared verbally and very little has ever been recorded in the literature, much of this "local" knowledge, the content of the whisperings, is slowly being lost.

Although much of this information has been lost forever, some is still available: it resides in the minds and memories of the oldest women in the community, the ones who were not caught up in the postwar era of becoming and being "modern" mothers. As these older women die, much of this oral knowledge is likely to be lost. Some will have passed some knowledge on to a daughter, but much will be gone forever. Without projects like this one, none of this information will be there when the young women of today finally decide they want to know something of the past, something of the old women's whisperings.

This small project based primarily on interview research conducted in Pohnpei in 1999 is only a faint whisper about women's things among women in Pohnpei. It is only a beginning and it touches only on a few aspects of women's lives, those directly associated with reproduction. It is only a tentative step toward preserving some of the knowledge that has helped shape, and continues to shape, women's lives and experiences and those of their children and their husbands. If we are to understand the issues surrounding women today, we need to understand them within the contexts of then and now.

ONE WHISPER OF A MOTHER

The following, an excerpt from a summary translation of a tape-recorded interview with two of the oldest women in the study, provides an example of the kinds of "whisperings" women shared with us. In this excerpt one of the two women is responding to a question about whether her mother had told her about menstruation before her first time. In it she tells us about her first time, how she learned about menstruation, and something about her associated beliefs at that time. Although this is only one woman's story, this short excerpt offers a glimpse of the candor of these interviews, of how freely women talked about their experiences and their beliefs. The woman told this story with much laughter and the frequent use of that very expressive Micronesian gesture of bringing her hand before her face, especially when she got to the parts she thought were particularly funny or embarrassing. This woman, like many of the others, saw the humor in her story and wanted to share it with us as only these women can. There were other kinds of stories, of course: some were sad, some were funny, some just were. It is through this variety of stories and reports of experiences and feelings that we begin to know something about the menstrual and birth experiences among women in Pohnpei across the ages, stories that we think reflect something of Micronesian women's experiences.

This excerpt is from the first few minutes of the interview. It begins just after a discussion of the study in which the women asked some questions about its purpose and after we had obtained verbal consent for participation and for taping the interview. (The tape recorder was never turned on until consent had been given.) The question was asked again. Although both women agreed to have the tape recorder on, one of them was still shy about talking, because she does not like the sound of her voice. When the question was first asked she rolled her eyes and made funny faces, and this made everyone laugh. She obviously had a story to tell, but she was not quite ready to tell it. It was not long before she began to talk, however, and although she continued to make us laugh throughout the interview, she was clearly a full and active contributor. In the meantime, her friend answered the question. Now that everyone had composed herself,

we asked again if they remember if their mothers ever explained to them why they bleed every month. They started out laughing. She stated she never asked her mother about this.

She is laughing out loud, saying that her experience was something she had been exposed to by older girls. When the older girls had theirs, she used to wonder where the blood came from. So when she had hers [she later reports that she thinks she was fifteen at the time], of course she was surprised, but she then imagined that it could be what she had already witnessed with the older girls. However, she was still puzzled as to where the blood came from.

When asked if she was not scared, she said that she was not scared because she already saw when it happened to older girls. Even though she did not know where the blood came from, she never bothered to even ask her mother, because her mother might question her about whether she was sleeping with men that she bled like that. So she just kept quiet.

People used to talk about people bleeding when they first encountered men; therefore, when a girl experienced first menarche, that was something they were scared of because they thought they were bleeding because they probably slept with men. So she preferred to remain silent about her experience until her mother found out by herself because this lady always preferred to stay home whenever there was an activity or gathering when she had her period. She would be tired all the time, not wanting to do anything.

We also asked this lady if during those periods she experienced any kind of menstrual cramps or anything that might signal the coming of her next cycle. She said she never experienced any physical or bodily symptoms. However, she realized that after her first period, second, and so forth, she expected to have her next period whenever there was a new moon.

We asked the other lady what about her experience. She said that she always experienced stomach cramps before she had hers. That was her symptom or sign to expect her next period. After she repeatedly experienced the cramps, her mother wondered what caused that. They tried to cure the pain by heating up/boiling water and soaking a piece of cloth and padded the area with it to heal the pains. The mother also began to believe that maybe if she got married that would help relieve her pains. During those days, they believed that if you didn't get married early during your early teens, you would be experiencing this kind of pain. Therefore, they decided it was best for her to get married. This was because they thought being a virgin implied the woman's private part needed to be penetrated and widened for cleansing. Therefore, in order to relieve or heal the pain, a young girl who experienced the awful cramps had to be married to break her virginity so she would be relieved from the pain.

This excerpt provides an example of the kind of information we collected during this project. In this project we used a form of ethnographic interviewing to elicit information on menarche, menstruation, pregnancy, birthing, the postpartum period, and menopause. The women were asked very general questions and allowed to answer in their own way. We also asked questions of expansion and clarification. Occasionally we provided a prompt or an example to help the women understand our questions. We even made contributions from our own experiences to give the intended sense of sharing rather than having the interviews seem like an interrogation. We moved on to new topics as they were introduced in the women's comments or as we ran out of questions or comments for the topic at hand. Some topics were not explored as fully as they could have been, as we let the conversation guide the course of the interview. The interviews were also constrained somewhat initially because I did not yet know how long women were willing to talk and what kinds of questions or topics they would be comfortable discussing. I soon found that women were willing, even happy, to talk about these things for hours and that few topics were considered off-limits. I was, in fact, probably much more cautious in asking questions than I needed to be.

On at least two occasions during the early interviews a topic came up that could clearly lead to a particular line of discussion. I did not follow up because I thought we had moved into areas that were too sensitive, and I thought the women's body language was telling me not to go in that direction. Later I was asked why I had not asked those questions. It turned out that the women had wanted me to ask. I had misread their body language. In these cases, what I had taken as reluctance was in fact a signal that I should ask a question, that it was a sensitive topic, but one she really did want to talk about; she just did not quite know how to initiate the discussion.

As my assistants became more acquainted with the kind of informa- ⁀
tion I was trying to collect and the interviewing technique I wanted them to use, I let them use their cultural knowledge, their knowledge of these individuals, and their own interests to direct the interviews. As we progressed, these women took on a larger and larger role in the interviews. They helped define the range of topics to be covered and whom to interview. I know that as a team we got more complete information than I could ever have gotten alone, even if all the interviews had been in English or I had been able to use their own languages with any fluency. At this point my assistants stopped being assistants and became partners in the research. There are still areas for which we do not have complete information, but again, this was intended to be just a first step in the process of collecting this kind of information. On the other hand, we probably collected more information on a greater range of related topics than I had initially anticipated. As already noted, the women were quite willing to talk about these things and to talk about them at length.

TALKING ABOUT MENSTRUATION AND
OTHER WOMEN'S THINGS

Traditionally women did not often talk about menstruation. For some it was considered a taboo topic, and others suggest that it was just something people did not talk about because it was personal and private. All of the women agreed (and some other informants support this notion) that talking about things like menstruation or other women's personal issues or revealing that they were menstruating would be absolutely taboo anywhere near brothers or any male in the category of brother. One older woman specifically asked us to please be sure her brother never heard the tape of her discussion with us because that would be very shameful.

This does not mean women never talked about menstruation, but such talk is rare and generally only among adult women, with close female kin and friends or a mother and daughter after she started menstruating. It was because women do talk about such things that they felt they could talk in terms of generalities; they were basing their comments on these discussions with, and observations of, others. It was also why the group interviews seemed to work quite well. This was not an extraordinary kind of thing for women to do. They might not do it very often, but talking about such things with a group of women was not unusual.

Today women may talk about topics such as menstruation somewhat more openly. Certainly it is discussed in schools during health education programs, and some of the women with teenage or young adult daughters said they have talked or did talk to their daughters about menstruation before the daughter started her menses.

The women who participated in these interviews were not hesitant to talk about menstruation or any of the other topics in the interview context. A couple of the women, one in her 20s and one in her 40s, seemed a bit hesitant at first to talk about using local medicines, but when we demonstrated an uncritical interest in local healing and its use, they seemed to speak more freely on that topic. Some of the women invited a friend along for the interview so they could help remind each other of things to tell us and, in some cases, for support. Some of the oldest women thanked us for coming to talk to them about these things. One group said they had really enjoyed the interview because it had been a long time since they had had such a talk, and they liked talking to us because we were interested and knowledgeable. Many of these women talked to us because they wanted to have information on traditional beliefs and practices recorded so women in the younger and future generations would have a way to learn about the way things were in the past.

Some of these women also had other agendas: they had things they wanted to tell us or ask us. Older women in particular wanted to talk about culture change and how it has affected life in Pohnpei and women and their health. Others wanted to obtain health information or personal advice. Most had a message they wanted included in this report. We hope none has been left out.

QUESTIONS ABOUT HEALTH

Questions about health and health issues were common during the formal interviews (for an example see the introduction to Chapter 7). Given the topic, the way the study was often described, the generally relaxed conversational interview format, and assurances of confidentiality, it is not surprising that some women asked health related questions, questions about their health and that of others. Women may have also felt comfortable asking these questions because, although few knew I have a nursing background, they believed that because I was conducting this study and had the title of doctor, I possessed special information on women, health, illness, and healing. Even though the women were told I was an anthropologist, a Ph.D. doctor, not a medical doctor, many still wanted my opinion or advice. In fact, I think the opportunity to ask me questions, whether or not they thought I was a medical doctor, was one of the reasons some women agreed to participate in the study (i.e., they would answer my questions and so they expected that I would answer theirs).

As with all women who raised questions associated with concerns about their health or that of others, the woman was first asked what she thought or others had told her and then I would share "what the scientists say."[2] If necessary, I explained again that I was not a medical doctor; I had a nursing background but I was not a medical doctor (psychologist, psychiatrist, or whatever specialty was involved). If her description suggested something worthy of further investigation or if a medical consultation would relieve the woman's anxiety about her health, she was advised to see a doctor.

Most of the questions were simply requests for explanations about very normal things, such as the normal age for menopause, or why women skip a period, or why the woman got pregnant while she was breast-feeding. On the other hand, with other kinds of questions it often became clear that the woman was seeking either a second opinion or a "plain English" explanation or clarification of a first opinion. Some had obviously already been to a doctor. When I could, I offered potential explanations and courses of action; otherwise I referred them to the appropriate health professional. I did not in any way lead any of these women to believe I was a medical doctor or had the credentials to provide medical treatment. I interacted with them as a researcher and educated health professional with specialized knowledge in the area under discussion.

The most important point here is that the interviews were based on a form of reciprocity: the women shared their specialized knowledge and I shared mine when it was requested or appropriate. The reciprocity at the time of the interview was not balanced, however; the women shared far more than I did. I hope that by sharing this report with the community and others, including the women involved, the exchange is now in slightly better balance.

DIVERSITY ACROSS AND WITHIN

The purpose of this book is to inform so that people may proceed in an informed way. However, no matter how common a belief or practice may be within a particular group, the information should not be used as a stereotype. Everyone within a particular group may not share the belief or practice, even if it is identified as a core belief or practice.

As expected, this project indicated both similarities and differences across the cultural groups involved. Some of these similarities are the product of sharing and interacting in the course of daily life. In some

cases this sharing occurs within families, because many families are themselves multicultural. The study also indicated that there were differences
in knowledge and experiences both across and within groups. This went
beyond differences across generations and included important differences
within generations. There were also indications that there may be some
important differences between those in rural areas and those in and
around the urban center. None of this is surprising, but it is worth saying at the very beginning of this book.

On the other hand, just because we heard about a particular belief
or practice from only one woman does not necessarily mean it is hers
alone. It might be unique to her, but it is also possible that we did not
hear it more often because we did not specifically ask about particular
beliefs and practices. We used informed prompts but we did not use any
kind of a belief, practice, or symptom checklist during the interviews.[3]
Furthermore, Pohnpei and all the cultural groups within it are undergoing culture change, so we would expect some variations in beliefs and
practices.

There are additional reasons this information is incomplete. To some
degree this is the product of all research. Even though we talked to many
women and often talked to the same women repeatedly and used other
strategies to obtain full information on these topics, we missed asking
some questions and did not know enough to ask others. But there is also
an important cultural reason for its incompleteness. As some of the
women noted, to give away all of one's knowledge, or to be asked to
do so, suggests that the person is no longer needed or is ready to die.
When a person does share "all" of their knowledge, especially in the
area of healing, it is generally shared with someone they select and often is kept within the female line. The preference is for the transmission
from mother to daughter, but it may be passed on to others. However,
even when people pass on significant portions of their knowledge, they
often hold a bit "in reserve" to be passed on just before they die.

It was quite clear to us that some of the most knowledgeable women
held some information "in reserve." We respect them for doing so and
would not have wanted to jeopardize their health by asking them to
reveal more than they felt was appropriate. Nevertheless, the information they shared was often detailed and extensive, sometimes acquired
over a period of time so all was not given at one time. We also talked
to a range of women, so we hope the information we acquired is not
too deficient in any way, but there is clearly still much to learn and much
to be recorded before this knowledge is lost forever.

It is important to note that although all the people involved freely
shared this information knowing that it would be shared with others,

it is still privileged information and should be used with respect. Nothing presented here applied to all women in Pohnpei, but it does provide a general sense of Pohnpeian women's knowledge and experience in the areas of menstruation (*soumwahu en lih*) and childbirth (*neitik*). We hope it can be used to enrich these experiences for all women.

NOTES

1. All quotes in this document are either direct quotes from interview transcripts (i.e., statements made in English during the interview), quotes from summary transcripts, or quotes recorded in field notes, unless otherwise noted. All the interviews conducted in a language other than English involved periodic summary translations in English. These translations are recorded on the audiotape. As noted in the preface, these interview tapes were then transcribed using the technique of summary translation.

2. I used expressions such as "what the scientists say" because I valued the women's explanations and wanted them to see that I saw these "scientific" or "medical" explanations only as alternative explanations. I also often told them that we did not know the answers to some of their questions, and that although we might have some ideas, we really did not know and that is why people are involved in this kind of research.

3. The format of the interview was based on interviews conducted in previous studies on menstruation (Fitzgerald, 1989) and birthing (Fitzgerald et al., 1998).

Chapter 2

Background

POHNPEI

Pohnpei, one of the four states of the Federated States of Micronesia (Chuuk, Kosrae, Pohnpei, and Yap), lies in the eastern Caroline Islands of the Western Pacific. The state of Pohnpei is made up of the high island of Pohnpei, which is subdivided into five municipalities and a town (Kitti, Madolenihmw, Nett, Sokehs, U, and Kolonia Town), and the inhabited atolls of Ant, Mokil, Oroluk, Pakin, Pingelap, Sapwuahfik, Kapingamarangi, and Nukuoro—the latter two are Polynesian outliers (see Maps 2.1 and 2.2).

Pohnpei State has a landmass of 133.30 square miles.[1] Its highest point of 2,595 feet above sea level is on the island of Pohnpei. Unlike the atolls, the island of Pohnpei is not surrounded by sandy beach, but by mangrove swamps. The temperature is nearly uniform throughout the year with mean highs in the mid to upper 80s and lows in the mid to low 70s. The humidity is generally very high on the island of Pohnpei, between 78% and 91%, in part because of the heavy and almost daily rainfall (350 to 400 inches of rain per year in the interior and an average of 194 inches in Kolonia Town). The atolls get much less rain, and as a result, the availability of fresh water is less certain.

Pohnpei has long been a multicultural community, particularly in the urban center of Kolonia, but its multiculturalism has become even more marked in recent years. This is, in part, because it provides the permanent site for the offices of the FSM government in an area called Palikir.

Map 2.1
The Pacific Region

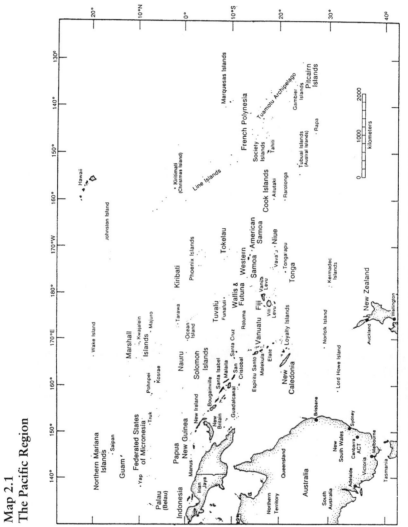

Map © Pacific Health Dialog, Resource Books, Auckland, New Zealand (2000).

Map 2.2
Pohnpei

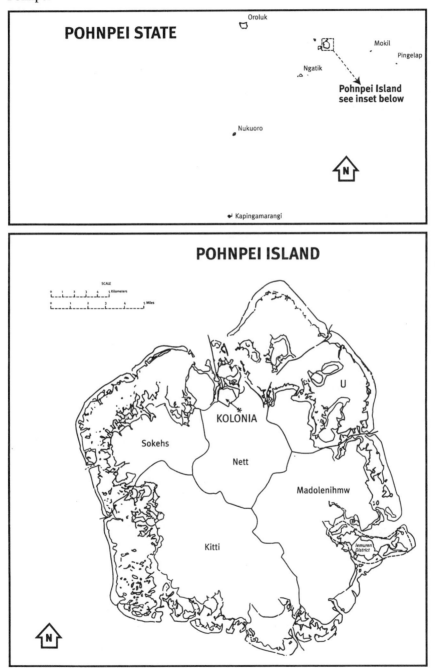

FSM staff come from all the states, and many federal positions are filled with contract workers from other countries. The staff of the Community College of Micronesia also make a significant contribution to the multicultural mix found on Pohnpei. According to one government report, the large number of English speakers reported for Pohnpei provides support for the idea that more non-FSM people live and work in

Table 2.1
Ethnicity on Pohnpei

Ethnicity	Number
Yapese	102
Ulithian	48
Woleaian	41
Satawalese	14
Chuukese	390
Mortlockese	936
Pohnpeian	23,372
Pingelapese	1162
Mwoakilloan	1203
Nukuoroan	541
Kapingamarangian	1037
Kosraean	368
Palauan	55
Marshallese	38
Other Pacific Islander	79
White	355
Asian	572
Filipino	466
Chinese/Taiwanese	34
Other	21
Multiple Ethnic Group	3,358
Total	33,692

Source: National Government Federated States of Micronesia (1996). National census report: 1994 FSM Census of population and housing. Palikir, Pohnpei, FSM: Office of Planning and Statistics, National Government Federated States of Micronesia, p. 185.

Pohnpei than in any of the other states (National Government Federated States of Micronesia, 1996). Although Micronesians, in particular Pohnpeians, still represent the largest segment of the population, the result is a multicultural community made up of people from diverse backgrounds (see Table 2.1). One FSM report indicates that at least 12 languages are spoken in homes in Pohnpei (National Government Federated States of Micronesia, 1996). On Pohnpei, 7% consider English their first language, with 68% claiming English as their second language.

In 1994 the total population of Pohnpei was 33,692, with a sex ratio of 105 males (total number 17,253) per 100 females (total number 16,439); 6,660 of these people live in the urban center of Kolonia (National Government Federated States of Micronesia, 1996). According to J.L. Fischer (1970, p. 292), in 1950 the total population of Pohnpei was "about 6,000," which means there has been a dramatic increase in the size of the population during the lives of most of the women involved in this study. Pohnpei now has a population density of 255 people per square mile.

In terms of religion the largest groups are Roman Catholic (52.4%) and Congregational (39.7%), with the majority of the Catholics residing on Pohnpei proper. The majority of the rest of the population belong to other Christian religions. Only 0.5% claimed no religious affiliation.

The median age at the time of the 1994 census was 18.2 years. More than half of the population 15 years or older (56.7%) were reported as married (married 56.7%, never married 36.4%, separated/divorced 3%, widowed 3.9%), a decrease from 60.2% in 1973. The average age at first marriage has increased from 23.0 years in 1973 to about 24.4 years in 1994. According to the FSM report:

> Like other population characteristics, marriage patterns changed also. Younger generations of both men and women tended to delay their marriages, probably to pursue their education. Additionally, with the change to more market economy, getting married, and running a family is expensive, so more women were in the labor force and contributed to the financial well being of the family. (National Government Federated States of Micronesia, 1996, p. 25)

The average household size in Pohnpei in 1994 was 6.3 people. Household composition has changed: it has "shifted from the traditional extended families to a more Westernized or nuclear family setup" (National Government Federated States of Micronesia, 1996, p. 25; see also for example Barnabas & Hezel, 1993).

The median household income in 1994 was U.S. $7,503, which is a 98.5% increase over income in 1980. Less than half of the population is employed (46%) and 45% is not available for work. The majority of this latter category are females.

According to the 1994 FSM census report, 94% of the population of FSM over the age of 10 is literate.[2] In Pohnpei 15% are high school graduates, but 13.5% have no schooling, an increase over the 13.1% reported for 1980.

Although a significant portion of the population is still under 15, there is evidence that "fertility declined during the 10 years before the census" (National Government Federated States of Micronesia, 1996, p. 11) (see Table 2.2). In a discussion of the age-specific fertility rates for FSM, one report says:

The reduction in the peak at ages 25 to 29 and the flattening of the curve suggests a decline in fertility. Although women aged 25 to 29 years are

Table 2.2
Fertility-related Information from 1994 Census Data

Age Group	Adjusted Fertility Rates	Average Number of Children Ever Born
10-14	NA	NA
15-19	0.080	0.190
20-24	0.221	0.967
25-29	0.213	2.339
30-34	0.163	3.421
35-39	0.118	4.577
40-44	0.047	5.270
45-49	0.014	5.913
TFR	4.274	

TFR = Total Fertility Rate

Source: National Government Federated States of Micronesia (1996). National census report: 1994 FSM Census of population and housing. Palikir, Pohnpei, FSM: Office of Planning and Statistics, National Government Federated States of Micronesia, p. 185.

having fewer children they continue to bear children into the later reproductive years, implying small effects of contraceptives on fertility behavior. A reduction in the early reproductive ages can be seen . . . these [changes] were probably due to the delay in marriage mentioned [earlier in the report]. (National Government Federated States of Micronesia, 1996, p. 31)

A Pohnpei State document says that the changes in fertility are not even across the municipalities, and that therefore, "The results suggest that the use of family planning services, female educational attainment, and female participation in the labor force contributed to differences in the level and pattern of fertility" (Pohnpei State Government, 1996, p. xxxiv).[3]

Table 2.2 includes the adjusted fertility rates by age for Pohnpei based on the 1994 census data. The reported total fertility rate (TFR) is 4.3, which is a decrease from 8.2 per woman reported for 1973. "The TFR thus provides a measure of the average number of children a woman would bear under a given schedule by the end of her childbearing years" (National Government Federated States of Micronesia, 1996, p. 30). In other words, if everything stayed the same over the next decade or so, childbearing women today could expect to have a completed family size of roughly four children. The highest TFRs in the Pacific are found in two other Micronesian communities: Nauru at 7.5 and the Marshall Islands at 7.2; the worldwide TFR is 3.3 (South Pacific Commission, 1994, p. 8). Given the current figures, the Net Reproduction Rate (NRR) is 1.9, which means that "each woman will be replaced by 2 women in about 28 years time (given that an average length of generation is 28 years)" (Pohnpei State Government, 1996, p. 60).

The information on the number of children ever born per woman suggests how many children a woman was likely to have had by the time she reached a particular age group. The last group, ages 45 to 49, provides an estimate of lifetime fertility. Thus women aged 45 to 49 in Pohnpei who finished their reproductive years in 1994 had on average 5.9 children. As noted above, the daughters of these women are more likely to have completed families of about four children. Fertility rates were lower for women with higher educational levels and for those in the labor force. The report suggests that

if policy makers want to lower population growth due to fertility, policies could be directed at increasing female educational levels and increasing women's participation in the work force. Also, given the high current age specific fertility rates, it appears that the uses of family planning which usually initially lowers fertility in the older age groups, is still rather limited. (National Government Federated States of Micronesia, 1996, p. 35)

The recommendation above includes the suggestion that to decrease population size, the use of family planning needs to increase, particularly among older women of childbearing age. According to Ahlburg, the prevalence of contraception use in the Pacific is generally low, "on the order of 10–30 percent of women in the reproductive age span, as compared with 49 percent for all developing countries." Ahlburg goes on to note that "opinions vary on whether the low contraceptive use among Pacific Islanders is due to limited access to contraceptives or to a low demand for family planning" (Ahlburg, 1996, p. 15). Because contraception is available through all dispensaries in Pohnpei at no or minimal cost, access is probably not the primary explanation for the low use of birth control (Pretrick, 1997).

Life expectancy in Pohnpei increased by five years between 1973 and 1994 and is now 66.5 years. The overall child survival rates in FSM have improved (1973 = 84%, 1980 = 91%, 1994 = 93%). Nevertheless, according to one report, the infant mortality rate (the number of infants under 12 months who die per 1,000 births) of 46 is still high compared with the rate of 33 calculated for "neighboring Pacific Islands" (National Government Federated States of Micronesia, 1996, p. 41).[4] It is also significantly higher than the report of 14 for developed countries (South Pacific Commission, 1994). On the other hand, it is lower than the rate of 74 reported for "all developing countries" (Ahlburg, 1996, p. 6) and the 82 reported for "less developed countries excluding China" (South Pacific Commission, 1994, p. 11). Thus, although the level of infant mortality in Pohnpei may not be acceptable, the South Pacific Commission summary statement for the Pacific seems as relevant for Pohnpei as for the Pacific as a whole: "the Pacific islands are well placed, having achieved lower levels of infant mortality than most other developing countries" (South Pacific Commission, 1994, p. 11).

HEALTH IN GENERAL

Table 2.3 provides information on major causes of death and some other community health indices. As with many Pacific nations (South Pacific Commission, 1994), there has been somewhat of an epidemiological transition from infectious diseases to the "diseases of modernization" or "lifestyle diseases" in Pohnpei. However, despite this transition, infectious diseases, such as upper respiratory infections, including tuberculosis, continue as serious health concerns. Nutrition is also a major health concern in contemporary Pohnpei. The nutritional status of the population contributes to health problems such as those associated with cardiovascular disease and diabetes, particularly among the

Table 2.3
Major Causes of Death and Other Health Indices for Pohnpei

	Major Cause of Death	**Percent**
Adults	Hypertension/Heart Disease	30%
	Cancer	13%
	Chronic Lung Disease	12%
	Stroke	11%
	Diabetes	7%
	Accidents/Injuries	6%
	Suicide/Homicide	5%
	Other	16%
Children	Prematurity	27%
	Pneumonia/Other infections	24%
	Malnutrition	9%
	Accidents/Injuries	8%
Other Indices		
	Percent of population < 15 years old	44%
	Birth rate	3.3%
	Total fertility rate	4.3%

Adapted from Flear, Samo, & Hezel (1998).

adult population, and malnutrition/undernutrition, which is associated with a range of illnesses found among children. In fact, recent work suggests that Vitamin A Deficiency (VAD) is unusually high in FSM, including Pohnpei (e.g., Auerbach, 1994; Hezel, 1999; Lloyd-Puryear et al., 1989; Sowell et al., 2000). The health concerns for Pohnpei are reflected in a statement in a recent report by the South Pacific Commission for the Pacific in general.

Lifestyle diseases, such as heart diseases, high blood pressure, cancers and diabetes mellitus, have reached epidemic levels in recent years, and are now the leading cause of death among most Pacific island countries. An increasingly sedentary life, combined with increased alcohol and tobacco consumption, poor nutrition (undernutrition in children as well

as overnutrition in adults) and some of the social and environmental factors mentioned earlier [e.g., poor education and housing, lack of access
to safe water and sanitation, overcrowding], contribute to the epidemic
of NCD [non-communicable diseases] across the region, and are responsible for a large proportion of the current morbidity and mortality levels. (South Pacific Commission, 1994, p. 10)

Despite the health concerns outlined above, all of which require attention, people in Pohnpei generally appear robust and healthy. They
are warm and generous people with a keen sense of humor. The concept of family and the importance of the family tie all the people of
Pohnpei together, Micronesian and non-Micronesian alike. The concept
of family may vary across cultural groups, even within groups, but the
family, however it is conceived, is important nevertheless. As Hezel
(1991, p. 1) notes: "Family come first, in Micronesia and just about
everywhere else." The core of all families is the mother. Becoming and
being a mother is, therefore, an important aspect of life in Pohnpei.

SOCIAL ORGANIZATION

Like many other areas of social life, social organization and social relationships are undergoing varying forms of transition in contemporary
Pohnpei. Some of these changes have been described in *The Micronesian
Counselor*, a series of occasional papers produced by Micronesian Seminar under the direction of Francis X. Hezel (e.g., Barnabas & Hezel,
1993; Rubinstein, 1994; Marcus, 1991; see also for example Hezel,
1994a). Detailed accounts, particularly at the sociopolitical level, are
found in the large body of work by Glenn Petersen (e.g., 1984, 1989a,
1989b, 1990, 1992, 1993, 1995). See also works by David Hanlon (e.g.,
1988), Eve Pinsker (1997), Elizabeth Keating (e.g., 1998a, 1989b, 2000)
and many of the contributions to the volume on Micronesia by Kiste
and Marshall (1999). Kim Kihleng provides a very informative discussion of social life from a female perspective in her doctoral dissertation,
*Women in Exchange: Negotiated Relations, Practice, and the Consti-
tution of Female Power in Processes of Cultural Reproduction and
Change in Pohnpei, Micronesia* (1996). Works by Suzanne Falgout, in
particular her work on marriage (1993), add to this body of knowledge
(see Chapter 8).

Despite all the changes—and concerns about these changes—there is
still a core to contemporary social organization that makes Pohnpei
unique and Pohnpeian. Fundamental to this core is the concept of family
and the role of women in society.

Drawing on the work by Barnabas and Hezel (1993) we note that the Pohnpeian word for family is *peneinei*. However, although this word can be translated as "family," it can be used to represent several overlapping groups, such as parent or parents and children (the nuclear family), all the members of a particular household, or all the residents on a single estate. It can be used to refer to "the group of related persons, however large, who live in proximity with one another and function as a social and economic unit" (Barnabas & Hezel, 1993, p. 1) or those who are linked by some genealogical tie even though words such as *lineage* may more accurately reflect that latter situation.

Although Pohnpei is described as matrilineal (and was probably once strongly matrilineal and matrilocal (F. Hezel, personal communication, July 1999), at least since "German times" it is in many ways more patrilineal, with the "modern 'family' in the 1950s" described as "a patrilineal unit that included the father and mother, all their married sons, and their unmarried sons and daughters" (Barnabas & Hezel, 1993, p. 1), although there were many variations on this theme even in the 1950s. A married daughter often lived with her natal family for a few years after marriage (matrilocal) and then moved to live with her husband's family on their estate (patrilocal). Any one estate and any one household could be made up of from one to three or four generations. One parcel of land in the 1950s might hold anywhere from a handful of people to 50 or more. As a result of the dramatic increase in population size, these same parcels of land today might hold two to three times that number (Barnabas & Hezel, 1993, p. 1). These people, as a social, economic, and political unit, shared food, labor, land, and the care of children. The *uhmw* or earth oven was not only the focal point for the sharing of food, but also "the symbol of the family's solidarity. . . . Together with the *nahs*, or feast house, the earth oven was the focal point of the family identity" (Barnabas & Hezel, 1993, p. 1). The symbolic importance of food and the sharing and distribution of food cannot be understated. The sharing of food, now and in the past, establishes and reinforces social relationships (see also Keating, 2000).

Thus, especially in the past, women often lived in multifemale and multigenerational female environments. At one time, and still for some women, these would have been primarily her female kin. With the probable transition from primarily matrilocality toward patrilocality in Pohnpei, as seems to be happening in other matrilineal Micronesian groups as well, the available females would be primarily the husband's kin. There is some disagreement in the literature about how much interaction between females might take place on a daily basis, especially between female in-laws. Demory (1976) suggests that in the 1970s there was often little interaction even when dwellings were quite close, whereas Kihleng (1996) suggests that in the 1980s relations between females, particularly those who lived in close proximity, were generally warm, amicable, and supportive.

Today Pohnpeians still tend to live in patrilineal groups (Barnabas & Hezel, 1993), but there is great variety in living patterns with more families living in nuclear family households, whether or not they live on a shared plot of family land or a family estate. These nuclear family households have become increasingly relatively independent economic and social units. There are still ties to a larger *peneinei laud* (extended family) and *keinek* (lineage), but they have become less essential in day-to-day life. Wealth, in particular wages from labor outside of the family, and child care are increasingly focused on or within the nuclear family or household. The sharing of wealth and the ever important exchange of food still occurs but has become increasingly symbolic and focused on special events that signify social connections. These special events, in particular feasts (for newborns, funerals, the giving of titles, welcoming and departing, etc.), occur often, sometimes weekly, in Pohnpei (Kihleng, 1996; Keating, 2000).

Although outside influences have altered gender roles and power balances among many traditionally matrilineal groups living in Pohnpei, and men more often have the most clearly identified public persona, some cultural groups have maintained more aspects of matrilineality than others. Thus, for example, the Mortlockese women we interviewed practiced matrilocality. Most, if not all, of the women on the estate were related (sisters/aunts, mothers, daughters, granddaughters), and land and other kinds of wealth appeared to be generally inherited along female lines, even if this was unofficial, given the inheritance laws introduced during the period of Japanese occupation.

The point here is that women, and the female line, are important in most Micronesian cultures' social organization. Briefly, as Kihleng (1996) notes, the maximal unit among Pohnpeians is the matrilineal clan or *sou*. A person is related to all other clan members because they are descended from a common founding *ancestress*. Membership in the mother's clan is determined at birth, so a child readily acquires clan membership even if the mother is not married at the time the child is born (see also Falgout, 1993). Once established, clan membership is almost impossible to change, even through adoption (Kihleng, 1996; see also J.L. Fischer, 1970). This means that the mother's family, in particular her brothers (*uhlap*), have traditionally played a particularly important role in the lives of their sisters and their sisters' children. Today the *uhlap* is still an important person in the lives of women and their children, but many of his roles have been assumed by husbands/fathers in the more nuclearized households in contemporary Pohnpei. For some women (and their children) this creates a new kind of tension between the roles of sister and wife. To whom does a contemporary woman owe her greatest allegiance? Her brother or her husband?

People are expected to marry outside of their matriclan (Falgout, 1993), but according to Kihleng, the only serious repercussion for marrying a distant clansmate today "is the anger and ridicule emanating from gossip, which can actually be quite severe" (Kihleng, 1996, p. 94). Thus one of the clan's functions is to regulate marriage and provide assistance and support during various life cycle events, including marriages, births, and deaths. In contemporary Pohnpei, the nuclear family (*peneinei tikitik*) has generally replaced the extended family (*peneinei laud*) as the organizing focus of people's lives. Today, people may choose to participate only in those events associated with people with whom there is a particularly close or important relationship (e.g., particularly high-ranking members of the clan or more immediate kin).

One key reason for drawing attention to social organization is to note the traditional importance of women in Pohnpeian society. Women have traditionally played essential and powerful social, political, cultural, and economic roles in the community (for more detailed descriptions see Falgout, 1993 and Kihleng, 1996). As Hezel (1993, p. 6) notes, women "used to exercise real authority over certain areas of family and village life." In fact, traditionally a woman's greatest loyalty was toward her matrilineage, not her father's or husband's, even if she served her husband's family in day-to-day life. Women "had a strong say over land, among other things" (Hezel, 1993, p. 6), although perhaps not as much in Pohnpei as in other parts of Micronesia (F. Hezel, personal communication, September 2000). They often had considerable direct and indirect influence over decisions related to the kin group. Women may be losing or have lost much of their former power and authority, but many are trying to reassert it, and at the same time, they are finding ways to assume some of the power and authority in the "new" state and national government. They are using formal and informal women's organizations and their positions in government and health care to do so.

There are other reasons for raising the issue of social organization. First, the relationships and activities that result from such organization affect women and their menstrual and birth-related experiences. It determines who women go to for information and support and with whom they must not discuss such issues or who should not be involved. Another reason for raising this issue is that the social organization of Pohnpei (and many other aspects of social life) is undergoing powerful and fundamental changes and that they have occurred in a relatively short period of time, since World War II. The mandated relationship with the United States post–Word War II has been particularly significant in this regard, but other factors are involved and other cultural groups. Pohnpei today is multicultural and part of a global community and, like communities everywhere, is undergoing all kinds of social change—some for the better, and some far less positive. What is important is that all these changes have an effect on the long-existing female biological-social-cultural-psychological experiences of becoming and being women, women who menstruate and women who are or become mothers.

THE PARTICIPANTS

The central body of data upon which this book is based was collected from mothers, many of whom are grandmothers and some great-grand-mothers (see Tables 2.4 and 2.5). Data were collected during 14 interviews involving a total of 24 women (one woman participated in two interviews). The women ranged in age from 20 to 72 years. There were individual and group interviews. The group interviews ranged in size from a fluctuating group that involved a total of seven women[5] to groups of two.

The interviews were conducted in the women's place and language of choice with the assistance of one, or more often two, multilingual local people who served as interpreters, assistants, and collaborators.[6] Even when interviews were conducted in a language other than English, it was clear that most of the women, women of all ages, often understood at least some English. Thus some of the women would respond to my questions without waiting for translation, and sometimes they would actually answer in English, or they might interject or correct the interpreter while she was in the process of interpreting from their language to English. Interviews were conducted in women's homes or meeting houses on their homesteads, an office at Micronesian Seminar (MicSem), or an office in a public building. Some women chose to come to MicSem because they wanted an excuse to get out for a few hours, and some wanted to come because they were curious about MicSem—that pink building that can be seen from the causeway to the airport. These interviews were a social event for most of the women.

The women represent several Micronesian cultural groups (e.g., Pohnpeian, Mortlockese, Chuukese, Mwoakilloan, Pingelapese, Sapwuahfik) (Table 2.4). The majority of the participants identified themselves as Pohnpeian. Many of the women are from mixed Micronesian backgrounds, with several representing both the main island

Table 2.4
Overview of Interviews

Number	Place	Number of Women Involved	Cultural Group
1	Meeting house	7	Mortlockese
2	Office in a public building	2	Mixed - Belau/Mokil
3	MicSem	1	Pohnpeian
4	Woman's home	2	Pohnpeian
5a	MicSem	1	Pohnpeian
5b	School	2	Pohnpeian
			Note: Second interview with one of the women
6	MicSem	1	Sapwuahfik
7	MicSem	2	Pohnpeian
8	Restaurant	1	Pohnpeian
9	Outside a house	1	Pohnpeian
10	MicSem	1	Chuukese
11	Woman's house	2	Pohnpeian
12	MicSem	1	Pohnpeian
13	Woman's house	1	Pohnpeian
Total 14		24	

of Pohnpei and one of its outer islands. Most of the non-Pohnpeians were born on Pohnpei, and all have lived on Pohnpei for many years. The majority of the women were Catholic; all were associated with Christian religions, and several hold key roles in church-related and women's organizations. Four of the five municipalities are represented, but the majority of the women live in the urban or peri-urban area of Kolonia.

In addition to the more formal individual and group interviews, data were also collected during interviews (formal and informal) and casual conversations in a variety of contexts with people from many different backgrounds. These informants included men and women from the community, doctors and nurses (local and expatriate) and others in their

Table 2.5

Cross-generation Comparison of Age at Menarche and Age of First Pregnancy

Cultural Group	Age	Age Menopause	Age Married	Teen		20s		30s		40s		50s		60s		70s	
				Current Age													
				M	P	M	P	M	P	M	P	M	P	M	P	M	P
Belau				*9*								15					
Chuukese	45 years	Hyster 1998	22	*11*	na					12	22				17		
Mortlockese	60s													early teens			
Mortlockese	50s?		25										20				
Mortlockese	50s?											16					
Pohnpeian	45 years			*2x10*	—					12	24			15	17		
Pohnpeian	68 years	38												19	21		
Pohnpeian	71 years															?	21
Pohnpeian	Late 50s	46										15					
Pohnpeian	55	Early 50s	na	*10*					*12*			9	24=1st, 40=2nd				
Sapwuahfik	60	48	22	*16*				*9*						15	18		
Pohnpeian	23	Na	22			12	22										
Pohnpeian	20	Na	19			12	19										
Pohnpeian	60s	50s	30											18	30		
Pohnpeian	52	50				*1x17, 1x14*	*21= 1st*					17	21=1st, 24=2nd, 36=3rd, 41=4th				
Pohnpeian	72	50							*14*							15	24

Note: M = Menarche; P = Pregnancy. Informants' menarche and pregnancy data are recorded in bold, their daughters' in italics, and their mothers' in roman.

professional roles, and, on occasion, clinic patients during observations in the clinics and dispensaries being conducted for another study. Some clinical observations were intentionally conducted on days when women were attending for prenatal and antenatal visits.

Data from all these sources and information from the minimal body of relevant literature have been combined to provide a broad picture of the beliefs, practices, and experiences that constitute the whisperings of women in Pohnpei, particularly in the late twentieth century. As already noted, the information is incomplete, but should provide a base for more detailed studies.

NOTES

1. Unless otherwise noted, the statistics in this section are taken from the National Government Federated States of Micronesia (1996) and Pohnpei State Government (1996). There are some minor discrepancies in some of the numbers reported in the two reports.

2. However, comments offered during interviews conducted during this study suggest that even though most young women have attended school, many, especially in the rural areas, may be functionally illiterate.

3. As will be noted again later, one of the doctors interviewed during this study also suggested a fertility pattern across the municipalities. This doctor attributes this pattern to a mixture of ethnic and urban-rural/outer island cultural differences that influence sexual behavior and marriage practices.

4. There is a discrepancy between the two reports. The Pohnpei State Government Report (1996) gives an Infant Mortality Rate (IMR) of 42 per thousand.

5. One woman was present for the entire interview; others came and stayed for varying periods of time. At all times at least three women were present, but more often there were at least five. The shortest stay lasted about 10 minutes and this woman, one of the youngest, did not speak at all. All of the other women contributed to the discussion at some point in the interview. It is also interesting that some men were present during this interview, albeit mostly young men and often for very short periods of time. They came, listened for a while and then moved on.

6. These women played all of these roles—and more. Because it is difficult to find one term that communicates this complex role, I have tried to use one that communicates the primary role at that particular time.

Chapter 3

Menstruation—*soumwahu en lih*

In this section on *soumwahu en lih* (menstruation or monthly sickness) we begin at the beginning. As we did in the interviews, we begin with menarche or an account of the woman's first period and the beliefs and behaviors associated with menarche and menstruation in general. In our discussions we also explored how women learn about menstruation, beliefs surrounding it, some of the feelings—the signs and symptoms— women associate with menstruation and their responses to these feelings, age at menarche, and other aspects of the menstrual experience.

It is clear that the women associated menstruation with health and pragmatic concerns, but at the same time, they viewed it as a form of illness. This is because it is often associated with feeling states, such as "stomachache," that can be signs of illness, and at some point, these same symptoms become signs that something is wrong.

MENARCHE

Most of the interviews began with a request for the woman to "tell us about the first time you had your period." The story below from a woman in her 60s is just one example of the way women responded to this request. The story highlights a number of common themes in these stories:

- women often did not know about menstruation before it began;
- many felt afraid because they did not know what was happening;

- they generally tried to hide the evidence because, even though they did not know just what was happening;
- they often thought that somehow it was associated with sex;
- because sex was taboo for them at that age they assumed they would be punished; and
- mothers used knowledge of their daughters' behavior or other evidence to discover when their daughters had started menstruating and then explained that it was something normal and natural.

This story also includes a common explanation for why women menstruate and one of the most common explanations for why women menstruate earlier today than in the past. Embedded in this story, particularly in the discussion of changes in clothing, is the notion that there has been significant cultural change within the lifetime of many of the women who were formally interviewed.

She said that she remembered it was summertime and she had to spend summer on her home island. She was attending the Catholic Elementary School here in Kolonia, Pohnpei. That summer was her fifteenth birthday. When she had her period, she was very surprised and frightened. She did not know what was happening to her, and what she thought was to hide it from her mom and her relatives because she was afraid they might think that she already *eseiehr ohl,* which means "already knew men" or had sex.

When we asked whether people used to believe that women who had menstruation was the sign of sex, she said that it was her own thinking when she had hers because she used to see these older girls who had their periods had already been with older boys. So when she first had her period, she went and hid under a bed. She used to wear *likouti* or the "wraparound" lavalava,[1] which was the style at that time. She just took the edge and folded it up between her legs to use as her pad. At that time, they had no menstrual pads so all she could use were pieces of old clothes and the edges of her lavalava. She did not even wear skirts at that time because it was not the style yet, but she was able to hide her period the first time.

During the second time, her mother found out. She was unable to hide the blood, which was on her lavalava, so her mother found out and asked her, "Mary, have you started your monthly sickness?" She said she was very scared so she lied and said no. Her mom told her not to lie because she understood what caused her to bleed. That was when her mother started to explain to her what was happening and how to take care of herself so she would not embarrass herself if people found it on her clothes. Her mother also explained to her that it was good to have her period to clean out inside her womb, and that not all girls have their first period at the same age. Her mother said that it would depend on the girl's system whether she is healthy or not healthy. Her mother said that if a girl is healthy, she would have it early and that she would have it regularly.

The word *menarche* in English means the first menstruation. There is no comparable word in Pohnpeian or the other languages associated with this study. Menarche was not marked by any kind of ceremony or other special form of recognition. Nevertheless, menarche was an important event in these women's lives and they could tell detailed stories about that experience. It was not a pleasant experience for most of these women because they did not understand it, and therefore they imposed explanations on it, generally related to sex or illness, that made them afraid of some kind of reprisal.

In many societies when a girl has her first period she is considered a woman, ready for marriage and motherhood. To some degree this was also true in Pohnpei, at least in the past. Marriages did not take place or were not consummated until the girl began to menstruate. Prior to beginning to menstruate a girl was considered, and continues to be considered, too young for sex. In modern societies where adolescence has been prolonged and the readiness for a transition to marriage and motherhood is associated primarily with social markers, such as graduation from high school or university, the first menstruation is often seen as merely a step in the long transition toward womanhood. It tells people that a girl is biologically mature enough to become pregnant even if she is not viewed as socially or psychologically ready to have sex or assume the role of wife and mother. This appears to be the position of many of the people involved in this study.

Knowledge of and Learning about Menstruation

Most women indicated that they knew nothing about menstruation before their first period. Women from some groups, for example Chuukese and Mortlockese, suggested that this was essentially a taboo topic, mainly prior to the onset of menses, and that as a result, mothers would not talk of such things with their daughters until it was absolutely necessary. One result was that most women reported that they felt afraid the first time. Some were afraid something was wrong with them. As one woman explained, it was blood, and for her, bleeding was associated with danger or injury, so she was afraid.

One woman was convinced that this discharge was evidence that there was something abnormal about her. She was more ashamed than worried, so she hid this periodic but irregular discharge for several years. She told us that she even quit school because of her shame and the problem school presented for hiding her period.

There was another, more common reason women were afraid. Those who knew or thought that that part of the body was associated with sex or childbirth often felt embarrassed or ashamed, and some feared punishment for something they had not done, namely having had sex. One woman said she wondered if, while bathing, she had been too close to a man, maybe his sperm had flowed through the water, like a virus, and affected her. These women often hid their menses from everyone, including their mothers, and often did so for many months. Eventually the mother would recognize something in the daughter's behavior and would talk to her. She would tell her that what she experienced was normal, that she was now a woman, and that she could now get pregnant if she was "with" a man.

One woman told this story about a Pohnpeian relative who first started menstruating during World War II.

> During the war people lived in the caves. A young girl was living in a cave when she started her period. She found some old cloths to use as pads. But when they were soiled she would have to sneak out of the cave to wash them and then she would hang them on the bushes to dry. Later she would sneak out to collect them.
>
> One day she was squatting down cooking when she realized that she was wet. She asked her mother to take over for her, that she had to go outside for a minute. In those days they cooked so there was no smoke so the planes would not see it and bomb them. Her mother became suspicious of what the daughter was doing so she followed her and found where she dried her cloths. Later, when they were all dry, she collected them. The next time the daughter went to get a cloth they were all gone. She was distressed and went back into the cave to sit and figure out what to do.
>
> As she held out the girl's cloths, her mother said: "Is this what you are looking for?" When the girl admitted they were hers the mother proceeded to tell her about menstruation. To tell her that now she was a woman and if she was with a man she could get pregnant.

One woman, a Pohnpeian, suggested that the topic was not taboo among Pohnpeians, at least not between mothers and daughters, but that this did not mean all mothers told their daughters about menstruation before the fact. Some women did. These women, the ones who had been told, had a less frightening experience. One key informant suggested that such talk was not common, saying that mother/daughter talk about "sex" was generally avoided because there might be a risk of men, namely brothers, overhearing them.

Although most women reported not knowing about menstruation before it happened to them, some of the oldest women said they knew something about it beforehand, not because anyone told them about it, but because of their own observations. One woman said that when she was young they went around without any clothes, boys and girls together. Sex was something they knew nothing about, and as a result, being naked around others, including boys, was not marked as sexual. In this context everyone could tell when a girl had her period; they could see the blood on her. She said young girls did not wear any kind of device to collect the flow; they just let it flow and bathed regularly. It just was not seen as a big deal. Later she said that when they began to wear clothes more regularly (both as a product of culture change and maturity) they made pads out of old cloth, old lavalava.

Most of the women reported that now young women learn about menstruation in two ways: in school and from talks with their mothers. Menstruation is, then, not an unexpected event for most young women today. Although there is less hesitation about talking about menstruation among women, some women report that they still feel (or felt) shy about talking about menstruation with their daughters before they began to menstruate.

Age

One of the questions this project hoped to address was whether or not there has been a change in the age of menarche, and if so, whether that change affected the nature of teenage pregnancies. At the same time we collected information on menarche experiences, we collected information on age of menarche.

Women were asked to report on their age at first menstruation (age at menarche) as well as the age of their mothers and daughters, if known. Table 2.5 shows the ages reported by some of the women involved in these interviews. Data from the large group interview with the Mortlockese women were somewhat difficult to place on the table given the number of women involved, the format of the interview, and the fact that they moved in and out of the interview. We also have data from other, more informal interviews. Thus we have more menarche and first pregnancy data, but only that which can be verified from our recorded data is included on the table.

In general, women report that they believe the age of menarche has decreased. Women in the older groups (i.e., 50 and above) generally report ages of 15–18 for first menses for themselves and their peers, but there also were women who reported beginning in their "early teenage year" and one woman who reported she was 9 years of age. The exact age at menarche is somewhat difficult to determine, especially among the oldest women (60-plus), because reckoning age in terms of years was not necessarily an important issue at that time in their lives. Thus, although women can recall many aspects of the event, some of the older women were a bit vague about their age at the time; for example, "I was in my early teenage years."

One of the women interviewed her mother before our interview. Her 90-year-old mother told her that in her day, and probably at least until the time of her daughter's age (the daughter was born in 1937), the usual age was about 15, but that a range of 13 to 16 and up was considered normal.

In the next generation (i.e., 30 to 40), most suggested a range of 13 to 15 years as "normal." These women report that their daughters started much earlier, with a range of 9 to 13, with most suggesting that the average "nowadays" is about 12.

The youngest ages at menarche (9 to 10 years) are primarily associated with women who are now in their late teens or early 20s. When they were reasonably sure of their age, women in the older age groups (i.e., 60-plus) reported the oldest ages (16 to 18). When these women could not remember exactly how old they were, with one exception, they used terms indicating their mid or late teens. The one exception indicated that she was probably in her early teens, and possibly not yet a teenager. This woman also indicated that she married very young and was soon pregnant.

As noted above, generally the women believed the age at menarche has decreased. The three oldest women thought that perhaps the herbal "medicines" women in the past took for their health when they were young may have prevented menstrual irregularities and contributed to their generation beginning their menses later. This is how one of the women explained it:

> She believed that the reason why they never experienced irregularities of their menstrual period was that they always took/drank local medicines prepared by their mothers. Because of the local medicines that they took during their periods, they never experienced complications of their period. Also, they believed that the reason why they had their menarche at later years during their teens was because they were always taking local medicines which cleaned or purified their systems. This means that the ladies believe that when a young girl is menstruating that means her system is doing its cleansing. Therefore, during their time, a girl had her period later

than 11 and 12 years because their systems were cleaned by all the local medicines they used to take, therefore, they had their menarche later than 11 and 12 years. (From a summary transcript)

More commonly the women suggested that girls in the younger generation start earlier because young people are healthier and therefore, larger than in the past. This same explanation was also used to explain early menarche among women of their own generation. They also suggested that girls mature earlier when they are healthier, although some other factors may also be involved, including, according to one woman, the effect of additives in prepared foods.[2] However, at the same time, women talked about young people not being as healthy as in the past; they talked about young women being undernourished, if not malnourished. We will return to this apparent paradox in a later chapter. It is enough to state here that there is general agreement that the age of menarche has dropped, and that the data we collected would seem to support this impression.

One woman suggested that when girls started their periods earlier they were more likely to have sexual feelings earlier and more likely to be "wild" and less easy to control than girls who matured later. Although this was the only woman to make such an explicit statement about the relationship between early menarche and sexuality or "wild" behavior, this would seem to fit well with some of the points some of the other older women raised.

MENSTRUAL EXPRESSIONS

Apparently women in Pohnpei have not developed an elaborate euphemistic language to talk about menstruation. In fact they do not seem to talk about it much at all. When they do talk about menstruation they tend to use one of three related terms in Pohnpeian—*soumwahu en lih*, *soumwauehn sompung,* or *wiah alu pwong*—all of which translate as "monthly sickness." In English they generally use the word *period.* This does not mean women necessarily see themselves as ill when they are menstruating. In fact, they see menstruation as necessary for maintaining health. Nevertheless, they associate menstruation with some feeling states commonly associated with illness, and they recognize that menstruation generally occurs with monthly regularity

SIGNS AND SYMPTOMS

Some women reported that they can tell when another woman is menstruating: "You can tell by her face." They suggested that the woman looks paler, especially in the space between her eyebrows. Her eyebrows might also seem lighter in color, or thinner. The woman might seem tired or lazy. Other women seemed surprised by the question and would simply knit their brows and shake their heads no. Menstruation was something to be kept private and personal, so they would not know about other women. Another group of women, primarily those in their 40s, talked about being able to tell when a friend was menstruating by the way they behaved. "They are uncomfortable, short-tempered. Yeah. [Other two women in the group make sounds of agreement.] . . . [Speaks as though she is talking to her friend:] Ah, you have your period yet? It's hard to talk to you. You are so uncomfortable. Every time I talk to you, you angry." (All laugh.)

Some women said they could tell when they were about to menstruate. The most common signs were fullness of the breasts or "upset stomach" (cramps). One woman also talked about swelling of her abdomen. Other women, particularly older women, said they knew when they were going to menstruate by looking at the moon. One woman said she menstruated at the new moon and others said the full moon. Most women reported that their periods were very regular.

Women reported primarily physical symptoms during their periods: "stomachache" (cramps), backache, headache, and full or tender breasts, with cramps the most commonly reported symptom. A few women said they felt very tired and wanted to sleep a lot. Only rarely did women talk of things such as being irritable or short-tempered during their periods, and they were more likely to note such things in others than in themselves. One woman said this happened only just before her period. Once the flow started she was fine. A few women said the only sign or symptom was their menstrual flow; otherwise they did not feel any different or, as one woman noted, perhaps they never really paid much attention to whether they had any other signs or symptoms.

A few women suggested that when women were menstruating they tended to stay away from their husbands. There was no rule about not being near or sleeping with the husband, but some women just were not interested in their husbands at that time, and there was some suggestion that some women found their husbands a bit irritating around the time they were menstruating. (See Fitzgerald [1989] for similar statements by Samoan women.)

With the data at hand, there do not appear to be significant generational or cultural differences in reports of menstrual symptomatology with the exception, perhaps, of slightly greater notice among the younger women of affective changes. Compared with Samoan women, Micronesian women, as a group, seemed to report few signs and symptoms. Their reports are more like those from rural Samoa than those from more modernized contexts (Fitzgerald, 1989, 1990). In other words, they reported few symptoms and these symptoms almost always involved terms associated with physical feelings. A few women in the community,[3] in most if not all cases, women who have lived overseas, mentioned the term PMS (premenstrual syndrome), but no one talked about having it. Thus, as with the Samoans, we need to consider the idea that as women have greater access to Western models and ideas about menstruation, the way they talk about menstruation and the signs and symptoms they associate with it are likely to go through a transition and reattribution process (Fitzgerald, 1989, 1990). In the next few years women may more often describe menstruation and its signs and symptoms in ways that resemble those offered by women in places such as the United States and Australia.

One Symptom, Many Meanings

Reports of feeling states or symptoms are often "multivocal" (Turner, 1967); they can have multiple meanings, (e.g., Fitzgerald, 1984, 1989, 1990; Hanna & Fitzgerald, 1993). For example, a single symptom report might describe a physical sensation, an affective or emotional state, and it can be a metaphor for individual and social concerns and carry a moral message. Sometimes it is all of these and more, all at the same time. Discussions about one commonly reported symptom, cramps, suggest this is also the case among Pohnpeians.

In one of the stories presented earlier, the woman reported that when she was young and a virgin she had very severe cramps.

> During those days, they believed that if you didn't get married early during your early teens, you would be experiencing this kind of pain. Therefore, they decided it was best for her to get married. This was so because they thought being a virgin implied the woman's private parts need to be penetrated and widened for cleansing. Therefore, in order to relieve or heal the pain, a young girl who experienced the awful cramps had to be married to break her virginity so she would be relieved from the pain.

In another part of the interview the woman again made a connection between a physical sensation and a physical/moral state: severe cramps as evidence of a woman's virginity.

> She has a daughter who is in her 30s and is experiencing stomach cramps. She believes that she is still a virgin; that is why she is having these cramps. The cramps are the kind that she experienced when she was a virgin.

Therefore, these ladies said that during their time, they used to believe that when girls are still virgins, they experienced these cramps. She advised her daughter to go to hospital for a physical check-up, but her daughter said that she would rather die than to see a doctor. She is afraid and shy because she is still a virgin.

Some of the married women with children would disagree with this woman; they have been "opened" and are clearly no longer virgins, but they still have strong cramps.[4] This woman's comment is important, however, not because there is necessarily any relationship between menstrual cramps and virginity, but because she, and probably many others, believes there is—and her "proof" is that her cramps were not as strong after she married.

Thus many things can have multiple meanings and explanations. One explanation for cramps is that the passage is not open enough to allow the blood to flow easily and the fact that it is not open enough is then, in this case, seen as evidence of a woman's virginity. In some cases virginity—or more accurately, not being married, especially in a more mature woman—is viewed as abnormal and therefore needs some kind of intervention. Particular explanations lead to particular actions, but there may be more than one potential action. In this woman's case, it led to her marriage—a social solution for a physical condition or problem.[5] In her daughter's case it led to the recommendation that her daughter see a doctor—a medical rather than a social intervention. In the daughter's case marriage or sex without marriage were not, according to her mother, acceptable actions, as this mature woman is apparently not particularly interested in marriage or losing her virginity, even if not being married is considered rather unusual. There were other reports of women, not all of whom were virgins, with either irregular periods or extended periods of amenorrhea, who went to see a doctor. These women were, according to our reports, treated or were being treated with medications.

Response to Menstrual Symptoms

For the most part women do little in response to the symptoms they associate with menstruation. Symptoms such as cramps make them feel uncomfortable, but few are greatly distressed by such symptoms. Some report using local medicine or Tylenol for cramps. Some women also changed their behaviors and rest or decrease their activities around the time of their menses. For the most part, today and in the past, women's lives go on as usual.

Women may not respond to menstrual symptoms for many reasons. One of the most obvious explanations is that these women may not have significant distressful symptomatology. On the other hand, Pohnpeians are rather stoic when it comes to pain. As we will learn later, women do not cry out or behave in any way that might indicate they cannot deal with the pain of childbirth. Some seem to accept that these symptoms are just part of being a woman and they simply endure them: they will go away in a few days and there is little they can do about them anyway (for similar statements from Samoan women see Fitzgerald, 1989). Pohnpeians seem to save complaints of pain or significant discomfort for extreme pain or potentially life-threatening situations. Even then their complaints may be somewhat understated.

BELIEFS AND PRACTICES

The sections above have obviously already addressed some Pohnpeian beliefs and practices associated with menstruation. For example, this material indicates that among people in Pohnpei there is a belief that menstruation is evidence that a woman has become sexually active. Some people believe that severe cramps can occur if a woman is not "open" enough, and thus, severe cramps can be considered as evidence of a woman's virginity. One treatment for severe cramps follows from this belief and involves "opening" the vaginal tract or "breaking her virginity" through sexual intercourse, preferably within the context of marriage. Most of the people we talked to believe that girls today begin to menstruate at a much younger age than women of previous generations and that this occurs because these girls are generally bigger and healthier. Some believe this early menarche is associated with an earlier awakening of sexual desire. Biological readiness for sex, namely menarche, is not equated with social and psychological readiness for sex. Perhaps the more important and outstanding beliefs are that 1) menstruation is normal and natural and serves to cleanse the body of impurities, and 2) it is personal and private and as a sign of respect for others should be kept hidden. Some of these beliefs are addressed in more detail in the sections that follow. This section deals with some of the beliefs and practices that have not yet been noted. Women mentioned them when we asked if a girl or woman should or should not do certain things when she is menstruating.

Among the primary Micronesian groups in Pohnpei, menstruation was not, and is not, noticeably marked with restrictive (or celebratory) beliefs and practices. These kinds of beliefs and practices are more common in other parts of the Pacific, most notably among many Melanesian groups (for two reviews of such data see Buckley & Gottlieb, 1988; Fitzgerald, 1984). Yap, one of the states of FSM, until recently had a more elaborate set of beliefs and practices, which included a period of seclusion in a menstrual hut. I could find no evidence in the interview data or the literature of significant restrictive practices or the use of seclusion or menstrual huts in Pohnpei.

One key informant with extensive knowledge about Micronesia suggests that menstrual huts may have been more common in societies that were traditionally patrilocal. Because there is some evidence that matrilocality once was more likely the norm in matrilineal Micronesian societies, there may have been no need for menstrual huts. Women had plenty of closely related relatives to care for her during this time. As I have suggested elsewhere (Fitzgerald, 1985), menstrual huts may have served purposes other than placing "dangerous" "polluting" women away from others in society. For example, they may have provided a respite from mundane and often physically draining women's work and may have provided opportunities for the socialization of young women into adult female roles.

The women involved in this study suggested there was only one serious restriction. All of them agreed that talking about things such as menstruation or other women's personal issues or revealing that they were menstruating would be absolutely taboo anywhere near brothers or any male in the category of brother. In fact, women generally hide their menses from everyone except those with a need to know, such as their mother or any other woman who assigns daily tasks, particularly cooking.

One of the most commonly reported beliefs was that menstruating women should not cook or handle food; more specifically she should not handle food for her brothers. This practice is consistent with others associated with the brother-sister relationship, particularly issues associated with respect and the avoidance of anything "sexual" in relation to brothers (real or fictive). One woman suggested that women could cook, but not actually touch the food. More often, women reported that in the past when a woman was menstruating, someone else did the cooking. In multifemale households, particularly among those groups where women traditionally often lived with their mothers (e.g., Chuukese, Mortlockese) this was not a problem. Of course this meant that others could view the fact that a woman was not involved in cooking as a sign that she was menstruating.

Barnabas and Hezel (1993, pp. 12–13) note that sisters were

> supposed to conceal their breasts in the presence of their brothers and avoid leaving around their undergarments or other intimate apparel.

Brothers, for their part, had to avoid allusions to any sexual matters or bodily functions in the presence of their sisters. The relationship between brother and sister was almost otherworldly in its purity. These strictures were carried even further in the case of parallel cousins of the opposite sex (that is, children of two sisters or two brothers). The woman (*pideli*, or "taboo sister") was not even allowed to approach her male cousin or touch his food for fear that she might be having her menstrual period at that time. This seems to have applied even after death, according to one of the informants, for a taboo sister who attended her male cousin's funeral never even entered the house where the coffin was placed for fear of breaking customary taboos.

Barnabas and Hezel (1993) go on to note that much of this type of respect behavior is being "eroded" today. Some young people have never heard of the *pideli* relationship, and there is less obvious concern about previously taboo or improper brother/sister behaviors. As some of our respondents noted as well, brothers and sisters may talk about intimate matters, like relationships, more often than before. Brothers and sisters might also find themselves in contexts where in the past their dual presence would not be considered acceptable, such as in a local club or dance hall. Some women, mainly younger women, suggested they still felt rather uncomfortable in such situations, but they did not consider them improper. Older women generally had a different view of such situations and found them rather troublesome, as evidence of the "moral decay" of contemporary Pohnpeian culture (see also Chapter 8).

One woman reported that a girl was not supposed to visit the family lands during her first period because the plants would wilt or die. There was no problem with subsequent menses, only the first.

Among Micronesians it is generally inappropriate to touch another person's head. Nevertheless, women, close friends or relatives, often comb, braid, and otherwise groom one another's hair. Women told us that during their menses they would not do such things. They would say they did not want to do it, or have someone else do it, or they would quietly tell other women they could not touch their hair at this time. Women explained that this was being respectful toward others.

As with hair grooming, public displays of menstruation, such as blood on one's clothing, was not considered dangerous in any way, just in poor taste. Allowing brothers to see evidence of anything associated with a sister's sexuality, like blood from her genitals, would be viewed as particularly inappropriate. It might be viewed as evidence that the woman's parents had not taught her proper respect behavior, but little more.

At its most profound, and this is probably pushing the point, a public display—which was generally viewed as accidental—might induce other women to begin menstruating. A couple of women, both Chuukese and Pohnpeian, told us that seeing evidence of another woman's menstruation, such as a stain on her clothing, was a sign that her own period would soon start. "She said she does not understand why but her way of telling that she was going to have her period was when she would accidentally see another lady's blood on her clothes. Then she knew that pretty soon she was going to have her own period, too."

As this comment suggests, the fact that this woman might start soon afterward was most often considered a simple coincidence. In a later section I will suggest that there is no evidence that menstrual synchrony was ever common.

As noted above, comments about things like stains on clothing address issues such as personal hygiene and respect behavior more than anything else. Cleanliness, particularly of a woman's private areas, was always seen as very important whether or not she was menstruating. Women reported using various strategies to avoid unpleasant smells (and accidental stains) in addition to regular bathing. One of these involved the use of local medicines (see below). Women also reported various vaginal cleansing methods, including digital cleansing (the use of their fingers to remove secretions), and according to one informant, some women even use soap and a washcloth internally. Most women believed that regular cleansing of the milder types contributes to the woman's health and sense of well-being. One woman raised concerns about the effect of the harsher methods on women's health and wanted to be sure her concerns were reflected in this book. She made her point by telling us a story about a friend who had recently died from cancer. The friend had use soap and a cloth regularly, especially during menses, and the woman believes this was a factor in her getting the cancer that ultimately caused her death.

Although women believe that their private areas should be kept clean and odor-free, they tend to avoid submersing their private areas in water during menses, either while bathing or washing clothes, such as in the river, because immersion in water could upset their system. This is because women believe that the opening to the womb is open during menses, and that therefore, a woman is more susceptible to infections. This is also a reason women gave for avoiding intercourse during menses.

Thus, although there is no elaborate or restrictive set of beliefs and practices surrounding menstruation among women in Pohnpei, a set of beliefs does guide women's behavior and others' assessments of a woman's behavior. A "proper" Pohnpeian woman behaves in certain ways regarding her menstruation. Mainly she keeps the private, private.

Why Women Menstruate

We did not ask this question of everyone, but when we did we got similar answers: The purpose of menstruation is to "clean out the system," to cleanse the woman's body, in particular her private parts. Some women told us they were never told why women menstruate and never thought to ask. For the most part they were told that menstruation was normal and something women did naturally. For many women this was a sufficient explanation. The general lack of discussion on this topic, and the apparent reticence in the past to talk about it, suggests that there may have been few opportunities for discussion that would lead to or allow questions regarding purpose.

Although women may have said they do not know why women menstruate, it is clear that they believe that it is necessary for their health and that if a woman does not menstruate she will become ill (see also, for example, Fitzgerald, 1985, 1989; Khanna, 1999; Snowden & Christian, 1983 for similar findings in other parts of the world). This idea came out in two contexts. First, women mentioned it in the course of general talk about menstruation; second, it came up in both formal and informal interviews about birth control, in particular the "injections" (depo provera). One doctor said that because women become concerned when they do not menstruate, the doctor makes sure women about to begin the injections are told that they may not have a period and that this is OK, it will not affect their health. One woman who has been taking the injections for some time told us she had been told she might not have periods, and she does not mind. She misses neither the fuss nor the bother associated with her periods nor the cramps. Another woman, during an informal interview, told us she "sort of forgot" to get her depo provera injection on time. The first time she missed her appointment they tested her to be sure she was not pregnant and then gave her an injection, but when she missed the next month she just did not bother to go back. This woman, now nearing her delivery date, indicated that perhaps her forgetting was not totally unintentional. It seems she was quite happy to have one more child, and perhaps not having periods was of greater concern than she had indicated in earlier conversations with her doctor.

Why Menstruation Is Kept Hidden

Women of all ages made it quite clear that women should be careful that no one, especially brothers, should know anything about their menstruation. One woman indicated that menstrual blood was different from other types of blood. It would not be shameful for her brother (or anyone else) to see blood from, say, a cut on her wrist, but menstrual blood comes from a woman's private parts. It was quite clear in this woman's discussion and in that of others that menstruation is associated with sex and sexuality (cf Fitzgerald, 1985). A woman's private parts are her sexual parts, and as we noted earlier, bleeding from the vagina is associated with sex ("being with a man"). At menarche many women felt "afraid." They were bleeding from their private parts although they had not been with a man, and yet, others might think so. One of the strongest taboos among many Micronesians is the taboo against any reference between brothers and sisters to sex or sexuality. This is one of the major reasons women gave for keeping menstruation hidden.

Menstruation, Health, and Illness

Menstruation is clearly associated with health, in particular reproductive health. Despite the fact that menstruation is often viewed as uncomfortable, it is still viewed as evidence of health and as a requirement for it. The primary concern is not with menstruating, even though it is a mess and a bother, but with not menstruating without an adequate explanation, such as a potential pregnancy. Irregular menses is not necessarily a significant concern—although it can be (see Chapter 6)—as long as the woman menstruates periodically. Women, in particular girls who are of an age when they should be menstruating, become concerned if they do not menstruate. There is a concern, first and foremost, that if a woman does not menstruate she cannot get pregnant, that there is something wrong with her internally or that she is not "open enough" to menstruate, evidenced by the lack of menses. At the most extreme, there is a belief that prolonged amenorrhea is the sign of a life-threatening illness. In such cases, in particular with delayed menarche, every effort is made to stimulate menses, for example, taking local remedies, including those designed for general health, and visiting local healers and doctors. One of the strategies, generally a last resort, is to initiate sexual intercourse, generally in the context of "marriage" but not necessarily so, to "open her up" and stimulate menses. The bloody discharge after first penetration is generally considered menstruation.

Excessive menstrual bleeding can also raise some concerns, although few women mentioned this issue. R.L. Ward (1977) talks about "sinking canoe sickness" (*mehn wahr mwowi*) as excessive menstrual bleeding. With prolonged menses, like other unexpected menstrual patterns, there is concern about the woman's reproductive health. According to Ward, such bleeding is associated with being bruised during sexual intercourse "with several partners or during menstruation" (R.L. Ward, 1977, p. 67). Ward notes that it can also be associated with a "jealous spirit" wherein it is viewed as a form of spiritual punishment for sexual infidelities. More often, however, excessive bleeding is viewed as a natural rather than a supernatural illness and is considered an indication that there is a problem with the woman's reproductive health, her internal organs. Again, as with other breaks in menstrual patterns, a woman generally visits a local healer or a doctor for a diagnosis and a remedy. She may also be warned against infidelities, having too many partners, or engaging in other "unwise" sexual or moral conduct.

Changes in menstrual patterns among older women, including prolonged or decreased bleeding and other irregularities, can also be associated with menopause, something that is viewed as normal. One woman asked us if a recent prolonged bleeding episode could be a sign that she was reaching menopause (see Chapter 7). If this was the case, she was not concerned, but if that was not the explanation, then she wondered if she should be worried that perhaps it signified something more serious.

Local Medicine

The recipes for most local medicines associated with menstruation, childbirth, and women's general health were either widely known or were family recipes. Women told us that if a woman did not have a recipe all she had to do was ask her neighbors, because this information was quite freely shared. There were, however, some medicines and some recipes that were known only by local healers or midwives. Some local healers specialize in women's health (see also R.L. Ward, 1977).

Women informed us that there are local medicines designed to maintain good health, including good menstrual health, although they were more commonly used in the past. These herbal preparations were taken regularly in earlier times, especially during menses, to help cleanse the body and keep it healthy. One woman suggested that these herbal preparations were the traditional version of today's commercially prepared multivitamins.

The older women talked about "applying" local medicines to the vagina or vaginal opening. One of the words to describe this process is *kamwenge,* which means "feeding to." Two of the oldest women discussed the regular use of a specific leaf women inserted into their vaginas to help them stay clean, to help remove impurities, and to help the woman stay fresh and pleasant smelling. This leaf was also supposed to prevent backaches. It could be used at any time to cleanse the "vaginal part." We were told that "when the uterus is not in its right position, they believe it is not happy, and therefore, it has to be cleaned." At least one of the oldest women, well past menopause, still uses this leaf periodically.

There were also local medicines for the "stomachache" (cramps) that could accompany menstruation. Women learned about these preparations from their mothers or, in some cases, from a local healer.

Some of the oldest women believe that the regular use of local medicines has kept them and their families healthy and strong. They think that the "young generation do not practice taking local medicine that much; therefore, they are not that healthy." They believe that if the young generation took local medicines to supplement or replace the hospital medicines, they could be healthier. One of the reasons young people are said to be turning toward hospital medicines is that local medicines are time consuming to prepare. The following is from a summary transcript with one of the oldest women:

> She believes that women nowadays do not practice these things (the do's and don'ts that were strongly practiced during her time) anymore; that is why they are often sick, and they prefer to go to the hospital than using local medicines. She said that she never goes to the hospital for pregnancy and delivery. Never. She said that her children do not depend so much on the hospital either. One of her children is now age 35, but has never gone to the hospital. They only go to the hospital for treatment such as when they get in an accident. She has medicine for things like diarrhea, boils—mostly those common sicknesses that we normally go to the hospital for can be treated with local medicines. Sicknesses that are inside the joints that cannot be treated on the surface of the body are what she might consider to be done at the hospital. But still, she and her children and her grandchildren are depending mostly on the local medicines.
>
> For pregnancy and birthing, we have all kinds of medicines such as those we drink, we shower with or bathe with, we apply on the body like oil, etc. Nowadays, women prefer to use the hospital and the medicines so they can just bring the medicines already prepared and just drink them and do nothing else. We are getting spoiled and lazy.
>
> She has seven children who still depend so much on local medicines. There was only that one with one incident of an accident who had to use the hospital for treatment.

It is interesting that women talked in much the same way about the use of imported foods. They said that people used them because they were more convenient, that local foods take more time to prepare so people were turning away from them even when they were more healthful. These women also believe that young people do not respect their bodies anymore. They do not take care of them; they do not eat the right foods and take the proper medicines and precautions.

On the other side, some of those within the medical system believe that people are not only harming themselves with imported foods and a generally poor diet, but also harming themselves with the continued use of local medicines. One of the areas of particular concern is the use of local medicines during pregnancy, and most especially during labor (see also Local Medicine, Chapter 5).

Menstrual Protection

In another section I noted that one woman reported that in the past when a girl started menstruating she did nothing to hide or collect the menstrual blood. Most women reported a different experience, one that may be related to a different age and context. These women suggested that they tried to find ways to hide their menses and collect the flow. Many said they tucked their lavalavas up between their legs to collect the flow. This was generally not a very useful technique. Others made pads out of old cloth and either washed them regularly (old cloth was not in abundance when they were young) or buried them. These women either tied them in place or used pins if they had them, but most said something such as, "you just learned how to keep it between your legs." None of these techniques worked all that well and "accidents" (a stain on one's clothes) were common. Some women said they stayed away from public gatherings if possible so they could avoid such embarrassing experiences.

Younger women (40 and under) reported that they had access to commercially produced pads. Even then some kept a supply of old cloth or old panties to use as pads if they could not get to a store or the store was out of pads. The women who talked about them told us they really liked the new pads with adhesive strips. They thought their daughters were very fortunate to have them.

Some women in their 40s also mentioned tampons. One woman said that she tried one once when she was younger but that it was so uncomfortable, she never tried them again. Based on the available data I would suggest that very few women, particularly those over the age of 40, regularly used tampons.

NO MENSTRUAL SYNCHRONY

Although many women reported regular menses and associated their periods with a phase of the moon, there was no clear evidence of menstrual synchrony. According to the women we asked, women in the same household or women who spent a lot of time together did not, as far as they could tell, menstruate at the same time. The one exception was twins. One woman with twin daughters said her daughters menstruated at the same time. Then again, women suggested that they generally did not know when others, even those close to them, were menstruating. On the other hand, women across the generations told us that if they saw evidence that another woman was menstruating, such as a stain on the back of another woman's clothing, this was a sign they would begin to menstruate in a few days.

Particularly in the past when many women lived in small villages or somewhat isolated homesteads, this woman with the stain would often have been someone with whom the woman would have spent a lot of time. Thus, although the few women we asked reported no menstrual synchrony, there is some evidence that it may have occurred, suggesting that this may be an area worthy of further investigation.

LENGTH OF MENSTRUATION

Those women who provided any indication of the length of their periods suggested that their flow generally lasted three to five days (for similar reports for other places see, for example, Fitzgerald, 1985, 1989; Khanna, 1999; Snowden & Christian, 1983). In some cases we learned this from a direct question. In other cases, the information was provided in a more subtle way. For example, in talking about women not cooking during menses, one woman said, "Four or five days of the month this person will not have to be around the food."

Across the age groups, most women reported being very regular and always menstruating at the same time of the month. Older women often associated it with a phase of the moon. However, a few women reported having irregular menses and some reported knowing of others with irregular menses. According to one woman, her sister has had irregular menses for some time. After an assessment at the hospital she is on some type of medication to regulate it. One woman said she often skipped a month. At one point she did not have a period for three months. When she began to bleed she assumed she was starting her periods again, but her mother told her she was having a miscarriage. When her mother persuaded her to go to the hospital, the doctors confirmed that she had spontaneously aborted.

One woman told us about a friend who did not menstruate regularly. Because she often missed periods she did not realize she was pregnant and found out only when she visited the clinic because she did not feel well.

> One of my friends she, now she's 25 and she just had her first baby too. And she didn't even know she was pregnant. Because, for that kind of reason. She never had her period. Like she could miss her period for three months or four months. And then she had her period for the next month but the whole month. For 31 days she will have it. Yeah. So when she got pregnant she didn't know she was pregnant. She just thought it was one of those. The only reason she found out she was pregnant was because she was throwing up and.... She just couldn't eat some kind of food. And her husband told her to go to the hospital to find out what was wrong with her and then she went to the hospital and she had the, they told her that she was pregnant.

Because the friend was "fat" and normally had a big stomach she did not look pregnant even when she was six months into her pregnancy.

One of the oldest women believed that women in her generation "never experienced irregularities of their menstrual period [because] they always took/drank local medicines prepared by their mothers." Furthermore, it was because of this local medicine that women "never experienced complications of their period."

NOTES

1. A lavalava is a loose skirt made from a piece of cloth wrapped around the body and held in place with a twist or knot in the material.

2. I heard the same explanation, in particular the addition of hormones to animal feed, from an American woman in Washington, D.C., during an interview in 1981 conducted as part of the Hypoglycemia Project directed by Dr. Merrill Singer (for reports on that project see Singer et al. [1984, 1987]).

3. This statement is based on information acquired through casual, informal interviews.

4. Women in other societies also note that having a child does not necessarily affect the frequency or intensity of their cramps.

5. Similar information was collected during the research with Samoans (Fitzgerald, 1989) and is found among other populations as well. Among Samoans, marriage, or at least sexual penetration, could also be recommended if a girl did not menstruate. Amenorrhea, particularly primary amenorrhea (never having menstruated), was viewed as a potentially fatal condition.

Chapter 4

Pregnancy—*liseian*

The God of Thunder went upwind to Katau to visit his clanswoman.
On the way his royal canoe sank, but a sea bass magically turned a
taro flower into a needle fish, who saved the God of Thunder. He
gave her a sour fruit to eat and she became pregnant. She bore a
son who was called Lord Kelekel.

(M.C. Ward, 1989, p. 64)

Stories (personal and abstract) and myths, legends and tales provide
ways for people to communicate with others about important aspects
of life. Although people may expect personal narratives to be taken at
face value, like myths, legends, and tales, they are also often meta-
phorical and carry implicit messages. As M.C. Ward (1989, p. 64) states:
"no woman really believes in magical sources of pregnancy." People in
Pohnpei see pregnancy as an important aspect of life, but they do not
believe women get pregnant from eating sour fruits or having intercourse
with supernatural beings, although the latter might be used to explain
an unusual pregnancy or the birth of an unusual child, in particular a
child with an impairment.

People believe that women become pregnant as the result of sexual
intercourse. M.C. Ward writes that traditional practices associated with
pregnancy are "really centered on basic biological information, shared
experiences, and the love of babies" (M.C. Ward, 1989, p. 145).

According to R.L. Ward, people in Pohnpei see pregnancy and child-birth simultaneously as

> natural events and as illnesses which represent a danger to the woman's health. The term *mehn neitik* "birth sickness" includes the invariable as well as possible symptoms coincident with this event. Chills, fever, head-ache, nausea, back and abdominal pains, discomfort in urination, con-stipation, and other symptoms belong to the time of labor or the period shortly thereafter. The expression which applies specifically to the con-tractions of the uterus is *lih pahn neitik* "woman will give birth." For this phase of "giving birth" there are medicines to speed delivery. The term *ohn neitik* "childbirth hangover" refers to virtually the same pains as "giving birth" and can be substituted for this term. In a narrower sense the former has to do with difficulties which occur after the child has been delivered. (R.L. Ward, 1977, p. 68)

In the following we concentrate on the information shared during this project; however, much of it is consistent with that presented by R.L. Ward (1977) and M.C. Ward (1989).

FIRST PREGNANCY

It is clear that the first pregnancy was, and is, very special. Many of the behaviors, beliefs, and practices women described were primarily for the first pregnancy and childbirth. After the first birth, when women had proven themselves capable of carrying a pregnancy to its desired end, some of the rules and expectations became a bit more relaxed. Pregnancy was still a very special, generally happy (yet potentially dangerous) time, but the first was even more so—under the proper circumstances, such as a desired pregnancy. Initially at least, a pregnancy outside of wed-lock was not a happy event. According to these women, such pregnan-cies were viewed as a reflection of bad parenting and considered shame-ful. Some of the women claimed that out-of-wedlock pregnancies simply did not occur in the past—but if they did the girl and boy would have been married as quickly as possible.

On the other hand, some of the women interviewed had out-of-wed-lock pregnancies, and there are reports in the literature that such preg-nancies were not a great drama. The pregnancy was accepted and the child was simply incorporated into the mother's family and lineage with little fuss (Fischer, 1970; M.C. Ward, 1989). If the mother was not ready, or did not want to assume the adult role of mother (wanted to prolong the "premarital state"), the child might be "let out" or fostered by an-other, generally by someone in the lineage, often an older sibling (Fischer,

1970; M.C. Ward, 1989; see also Schneider, 1968 in regards to Yap).[1] If such agreements were entered into too quickly and/or involved an adoption that resulted in a complete separation from the child (e.g., adoption outside of the lineage or to a non-Pohnpeian), the mother might be accused of "throwing away her child" (see also Fischer, 1970).

Age

As noted earlier, there was almost unanimous agreement that women are having babies younger than in the past—and that there are more teenage pregnancies. The one exception was an older woman who indicated that she was in her early teens and possibly not yet a teen when she had her first menses and that she had her first pregnancy about two years later. This would mean that she may have been, as she reported, in her "early teenage years" at her first pregnancy. Nevertheless, she too indicated that she felt that there were more girls having babies at younger ages than in the past. A woman who reported on her interview with her 90-year-old mother reported that her mother thought that in the past some girls started their first menstrual periods "something like 13 years and some even start having their first pregnancy [then]." If women are menstruating earlier then it is certainly possible, even likely, even if there is a period of adolescent sterility,[2] that there are more pregnancies at a younger age.

Women were asked to report on their age at first pregnancy as well as the age of their mothers and daughters. Reported ages varied from 15 to 30 years of age (see Table 2.5). The ages women reported for their mothers may represent first live birth rather than first pregnancy, because I suggested they use the age of their oldest sibling as a way to guess the mother's age when it was not known. In several cases the women already knew the answer to this question, because they had either discussed this with their mothers at some point in the past, or asked them in preparation for this interview. The women felt confident that they knew the age of their daughters' first pregnancies.

Teen Pregnancies

In recent years there has been some publicly expressed concern about "teen pregnancies" in Pohnpei. Prior to beginning the study, I was told that there was a belief in the community that more young women were getting pregnant in their "early teenage years," that this was a new phenomenon, and it was considered a serious health and social issue. Thus, when I proposed this study, I was asked to include the collection of information that might address this concern. In fact, this request was one of the reasons this study was expanded to cover the whole reproductive cycle.

Only later did I realize what people meant when they talked about "teen pregnancies." The data from our interviews and discussions with people in the community suggest that when people talk about teenage pregnancies or say that girls are getting pregnant earlier today than in the past, they are not talking about 15- to 19-year-olds. The age group commonly cited in statistics on teen pregnancies is in places like the United States—my reference point. What they seemed to be talking about were pregnancies among girls under 15, even as young as 12 or under, what they referred to as the "early teenage years." In other cases, they seemed to be talking about pregnancies among teenagers who were not married regardless of age. Although the concerns were often expressed in terms of the health consequences of teen pregnancy on the young mother and her child (generally based on studies from the United States), often these expressed concerns appeared to relate as much to concerns about sexual behavior among teenagers and the social consequences of becoming a mother at a young age in contemporary Pohnpei (see Chapter 8).

Data complied by Dr. Joseph Flear using the PIHOA (Pacific Island Health Officers Association) database provides information on age at first delivery for the years 1991–1994 (personal communication, May 1999) (Table 4.1). During that four-year period there were 4,069 deliveries of which 11 were among women 10 to 14 years of age (0.2%) and 752 (18.5%) were among women aged 15 to 19. The total for all teen pregnancies (10 to 19 years of age) for that four-year period is then 763 or 18.8% (18–20% of all pregnancies per year). According to the 1996 Pohnpei State Census Report, in 1994 the adjusted age specific fertility rate (ASFR) for 15 to 19 year olds was 0.080. Clearly the birth rate among 10- to 14-year-olds is even lower, with the highest number of reported births being 17 in 1989, and 0 to 4 in the other years for which I have data. According to a Pacific Basin Maternal and Child Health Resource Center (PBMCH) report published in 1996, the national goal for all of FSM was to reduce "teen pregnancy (<17 years)" from 50 per 1,000 to 25 per 1,000 by the year 2000; the rate reported for 1995 for all of the FSM was 28 per 1000.

Data from an earlier period (1986–1989) are taken from a government report (Government of the Federated States of Micronesia, 1990). These data suggest an unusually large number of deliveries (17 compared with two to four in other years) among females below the age of 15 in 1989 for which there is no offered explanation (Table 4.1).[3] If these

Table 4.1
Age at First Delivery for Pohnpei 1986–1989*, 1991–1994**

Age Group	1986 N	1986 %	1987 N	1987 %	1988 N	1988 %	1989 N	1989 %	1991 N	1991 %	1992 N	1992 %	1993 N	1993 %	1994 N	1994 %
10-14	2	0.2	6	0.6	0	0.0	17	1.6	4	0.4	2	0.2	3	0.3	2	0.2
15-19	160	15.9	153	15.6	151	16.3	164	15.7	170	17.5	186	18	189	18.8	207	19.5
20-24	333	33.1	307	31.4	328	35.3	314	30.0	341	35.2	346	33.5	338	33.6	340	32.1
25-29	249	24.7	275	28.1	248	26.7	273	26.1	212	21.9	237	22.9	228	22.7	265	25
30-34	156	15.5	150	15.3	133	14.3	186	17.8	142	14.6	170	16.5	151	15	159	15
35-39	74	7.3	59	6.0	48	5.2	74	7.1	74	7.6	75	7.3	78	7.8	74	7
40-44	20	2.0	15	1.5	13	1.4	18	1.7	26	2.7	17	1.6	19	1.9	11	1
45-49	4	0.4	1	0.1	0	0.0	1	0.1	1	0.1	0	0	0	0	1	0.1
Unknown	9	0.9	12	1.2	7	0.8	0	0.0	0	0	0	0	0	0	1	0.1
Total all	1007	100.0	978	100.0	928	100.0	1047	100.0	970	100.0	1033	100	1006	100.1	1060	100
All 10-19 year olds	162	16.1	159	16.3	151	16.3	181	17.3	174	17.9	188	18.2	192	19.1	209	19.7

Adapted from:
*Government Federated States of Micronesia (1990). Digest of Health Statistics 1990. Pohnpei, FSM: Government of the Federated States of Micronesia Department of Human Resources Medical and Vital Statistics Office.
**Personal communication, Joseph Flear, May 1999, compiled from PIHOA database.

figures are accurate, they may help explain why people believe there has been an increase in the number of teenage pregnancies in contemporary Pohnpei has increased even though other information suggests that there may not be an actual increase in "teenage" pregnancies. Many women indicated that in the past pregnancies were common among women in their mid to late teens (see also Table 2.5). If this is the case then it is unlikely that there is an actual increase in "teenage pregnancies"—if the term "teenage pregnancies" includes women from 13 to 19 years of age.

A report by Henshaw (1999) for the United States indicates that the pregnancy rate among U.S. women aged 14 or younger in 1994 was 15.8 per 1,000, and in 1996 13.3 per 1,000 with a birthrate in 1994 at 7.1 per 1,000 and 6.0 per 1,000 in 1996. For 1986, the earliest year for which I have data for Pohnpei, the U.S. rate was 17.3 pregnancies per 1,000 with a birthrate of 6.0 per 1,000. The Henshaw report indicates that in the United States there were 106.1 pregnancies per 1,000 in 1994 and 97.3 per 1,000 in 1996 for women aged 15 to 19. There were 91.5 births per 1,000 in 1994 and 54.4 per 1,000 women in 1996 in the same age group. In Hawaii the rate of pregnancies among 15- to 19-year-olds was 101 per 1,000 with a birthrate of 48 per 1,000 women aged 15 to 19.

Local meanings and concerns were reported by several women having heard of a 12-year-old who got pregnant. Two of the oldest women asked to talk about one of these 12-year-olds. First they told us they had trouble believing that a girl as young as 12 could get pregnant or could safely deliver a baby. They did not think that she could be physically mature enough. They asked if a 12-year-old could have pubic hair yet. In the case they were discussing, the girl and her baby reportly died at the time of the delivery. They said the girl had trouble delivering the baby so they "cut her" to get it out, but both died. The idea of girls this young getting pregnant was very distressful. They associated such situations with the kinds of dramatic changes they had seen in their lifetimes. Like other women involved in the study, they were sure girls were menstruating earlier because they were bigger, and therefore, potentially able to get pregnant, but they still had trouble believing they could actually get pregnant that early—and if they could, this was just too dangerous a situation. It was just one more piece of evidence of the "moral decay" of modern society (see also Chapter 8).

As noted above, the number of pregnancies among teenagers in Pohnpei in recent years is not out of proportion to the numbers reported for the United States. Of course these figures could still represent an increase in pregnancies among girls in their early teens for Pohnpei, particularly if the age of menarche has in fact decreased. However, our data suggest that teenage pregnancies have a long history in Pohnpei, that it was not uncommon for 15-year-olds to get pregnant and that in fact, many of these 15-year-olds were also often married. In our interviews and discussions in the community, stories about 12-year-olds getting pregnant began to take on mythical proportions and sound like an "urban myth"—and like all urban myths, these stories had a moral message. Again, like many urban myths, there is often some basis for the original story, but then the stories sort of take on a life of their own. The number of births among girls under 15 in 1989 might be sufficient to get such stories started. The death of one 12-year-old could also be sufficient. Just one death in 1989 of one 12-year-old could provide a rather substantial basis for a story that touches on critical community issues.

However, none of the health professionals I interviewed knew of a 12-year-old who was pregnant in the last 10 years, let alone one who died. The youngest any of them reported was a 13-year-old, but according to one informant she had not yet given birth. It is possible the women were talking about a case that occurred more than 10 years ago, which would be beyond the era for which these informants could report; in fact, data from the interview transcripts suggests this may have happened in the early 1980s. On the other hand, several health professionals report on a case from the mid-1990s of a "sophomore" in high school (age about 15 years) who got pregnant. She died from complications after delivery; the baby died a few months later of what may have been a congenital defect. One of the informants reported that in the community, people said the baby died because his mother's spirit came to claim her child. The current stories about pregnant 12-year-olds may involve a confounding of several cases or they may be unrelated to any actual case. They most certainly carry a moral tale.

SIGNS AND SYMPTOMS

When women were asked how they knew when they were pregnant often one of the first answers was that they felt sick and threw up all the time, and could not keep any food in them except maybe "sour" fruits for the first few months. The story about Lord Kelekel reported by M.C. Ward (1989, see the excerpt above) makes an association between pregnancy and sour fruit, which may or may not have any relationship to these women's discussions of sour fruit during pregnancy. The women did not make such a connection, but a lifetime of knowledge of this story might have some influence. The next most common sign was the cessation of menses. Several women also mentioned fullness of the breasts.

A few women admitted that they did not know when they were pregnant, or at least not the first time. They found out when their sister, sister-in-law, mother, or mother-in-law told them—or, in a case reported earlier, from a doctor when she went to the clinic complaining of not feeling well.

These other women used a variety of signs as indicators of pregnancy. Some women reported that they could tell when another woman was pregnant by looking at her face. As with menses it was the color of the face, especially between the eyebrows, and the pale color and lack of fullness in the eyebrows themselves. Others "suspected she might be pregnant because she began to crave for certain foods, and she seemed to be very lazy."

One woman, who became pregnant when she was not married, told us this story:

> Her mother asked her if she was pregnant. She said no. The mother was sure her daughter was pregnant, but the girl kept denying it. At first she really did not know she was pregnant. But about this time, four months into her pregnancy, she began to think her mother might be right. Her mother needed evidence of the pregnancy so she asked the girl's friend to get into a situation where she could see her friend's breasts. If her nipples and the area around them were dark brown then it was a positive sign she was pregnant. The friend tried to get the girl to shower with her, a common practice among young women, sisters, and friends. But the girl would not let her friend come into the shower area with her so the friend peeked over the top of the wall when the girl was undressed. She then went off and told the girl's mother that yes, her nipples were brown, she was pregnant. The girl's mother confronted the girl with this news. The girl felt very ashamed. She had dishonored the family. She told her mother that she wanted to get rid of the baby. Her mother told her no. Getting pregnant without a husband was wrong and shameful, but it would be a greater shame to get rid of the baby. The family would take care of her and the baby. (Summary from a transcript)

One woman said her mother-in-law always knew she was pregnant before she did. Her mother-in-law would tell her that she wanted to check to be sure. The woman would lie down and her mother-in-law would massage her stomach. She said her mother-in-law could tell from her massage whether she was pregnant, because she could feel a mass. Apparently this was a skill that other women possessed also. Some of them were recognized as local healers, particularly in the area of women's health. Among this group of women were those considered especially skilled at predicting the sex of the unborn child.

FOOD AND ODD CRAVINGS

Although this is not necessarily viewed as a "symptom" of illness or pregnancy, women reported that they often had cravings for certain foods when they were pregnant. One of the most commonly mentioned was sour fruits. In line with the report by R.L. Ward (1977, p. 69), these "pregnancy cravings" (*inengern liseian*) could include an "appetite for odd foods." According to Ward this behavior was not viewed as an illness, but as something caused by pregnancy. The usual response was to give the woman what she asked for. In fact, according to the women involved in this study, it was potentially dangerous to deny a pregnant woman anything she craved.

Two of the older women volunteered that they had some unusual or particularly odd cravings when they were pregnant. "One thing she liked to smell was the electric posts. She would go and stand by the electric post just to smell its odor. The other lady said she used to like the smell of gasoline. She used to sniff it."

Pica, the craving and consumption of nonfood items or "non-nutrional substances" (American Psychiatric Association, 1994; see Rose, Porcerelli, & Neale, 2000, for a recent review of the literature on pica), is found worldwide and "has no barriers of age, race, sex or geographical region" (Savetta, 1986, p. 181). It is common among pregnant women in many places. It is most often related to the desire to consume nonfood substances such as dirt, clay, or ice cubes. DSM-IV (*Diagnostic and Statistical Manual of Mental Disorders*, fourth edition, American Psychiatric Association, 1994) treats pica as a disorder if it lasts at least one month.

Although the reason people ingest such substances is not clear, some suggest the pica substances may provide things missing or inadequate in the woman's diet, such as necessary minerals, particularly iron. On the other hand, pica can result in a number of serious health problems, depending on the substance and the amount ingested. Cravings for foods such as sour fruits might address a nutritional need and are unlikely to have negative health consequences.

The cravings of the two women mentioned above might also be classified as pica, although they are unusual because they did not involve ingestion of any substances. Cooksey (1995, p. 129) recently described the "olfactory cravings of pregnancy" as "a previously unnamed practice" and notes that it probably often goes unreported to health professionals. Cooksey suggest that these cravings may occur alone or with pica and that perhaps we can consider them a form of pica.

In the two olfactory cases reported here, the cravings posed a potential risk for both the mother and the developing child. These women saw these behaviors as odd and silly, but apparently they did not view them as risky, and at that time even health professionals might not have been fully aware of the risks involved in inhaling such substances because little was known about the practice or its effect until recently (Marshall, Sexton, & Insko, 1994, 1996). The works by Marshall, Sexton, and Insko on gasoline sniffing and inhalant abuse in FSM notes the use, especially among children and adolescents, and its potential ill effects, but does not mention its use among pregnant women. Information from the current study suggests, and only suggests, that this behavior may have had an effect on the children involved, an effect consistent with what we now know to be the potential effects of gasoline sniffing.

One day we saw a man walking down the road, and one of the team said he was the son of one of the women referred to above. He was described as a "bit off" and apparently this description could be applied to a couple of his siblings as well. We do not know whether this woman sniffed gasoline during these pregnancies, but if she did, this behavior might help explain the disabilities among her children.

BELIEFS AND PRACTICES

In many societies pregnancy is surrounded by a variety of taboos or special beliefs and practices designed to enhance the pregnancy experience or to prevent bad things, such as death or permanent disablement of the mother or the child. As Ashby notes in a reference to Pingelap, "all of these [beliefs and practices] exist for the health of the expectant mother and her unborn baby" (Ashby, 1983b, p. 31).

Reviews of the literature and casual discussions with local women, especially with young women, suggest that Pohnpei was unusual in terms of the relatively low amount of elaboration of beliefs and practices during this important stage in the life cycle. However, as the interviews unfolded, women began to talk more freely about these beliefs and practices, and although still rather unelaborated compared with many other societies, there is clearly a body of specialized knowledge, beliefs, and practices related to pregnancy. I suspect that these interviews may have touched only on some of these beliefs and practices and their transformations over the years. Perhaps this account will encourage women to complete the record.

Ashby (1983a, 1983b), one of the few to provide any information on these beliefs and practices, says, "Ponapeans practice certain customs before and after the birth of a first-born baby. Some of these are traditional and have been practiced for many years, and some are of recent origin" (Ashby, 1983b, p. 26).

He notes in a reference to Mokil that such beliefs and practices applied to "all babies and not only to the first-born" (Ashby, 1983b, p. 29). It is not clear from the interviews conducted as part of this study whether these discussions were for only firstborns or for all children. Because the women represented several groups on Pohnpei and talked in terms of a roughly 50-year period, in some cases this may have applied only to firstborns. But there are indications that many of the reported beliefs and practices applied to all pregnancies; they may just have been more elaborate for the first.

Table 4.2 presents a list of beliefs and practices compiled by Ashby, which he called "Superstitions, Omens and Taboos." Most were also recorded during this study.

Treated Like a Queen

Two of the people who have written about the beliefs and practices associated with pregnancy in Pohnpei, Ashby (1983a, 1983b) and M.C. Ward (1989), note that the family catered to the expectant woman's every need and desire.

In this excerpt from Martha Ward's book (1989), she is referring to two of her research colleagues: her husband, Roger Ward, and the project director, John Fischer. Both of these men wanted Martha, who was pregnant at the time, to use her pregnancy as a "great opportunity for collecting data" (M.C. Ward, 1989, p. 144) on indigenous medicine and mythology and social structure.

> Neither believed me when I extolled the virtues of coconut oil, massage, and female support systems. Nor were they interested in lectures I had received on the customs of catering to the every whim of a pregnant women [*sic*]. Pohnpeian husbands and relatives are expected to arise in the middle of the night and fix foods a pregnant woman craves and needs for the baby's growth. Attention to the arbitrary and strong-minded desires of a pregnant wife take precedence over regular routines and career advancement and should increase with birth and continue during nursing. (M.C. Ward, 1989, p. 145)

Ashby notes: "Expectant mothers, especially those having their first child, are treated with great care on Pohnpei, and are never left alone. They are provided with anything they desire. It is thought that failure to do so would cause the expectant mother to have great pain in childbirth" (Ashby, 1983a, p. 188).

More so in the past than today, a pregnant woman was "treated like a queen." Her every wish was to be catered to. If she wanted some

Table 4.2
Superstitions, Omens and Taboos

- If food is not cooked well in a traditional oven (*uhmw*), it means that the wife is pregnant.
- It is bad luck for a pregnant woman to wear flowers.
- When traveling, a pregnant woman should always have a cover on her head.
- A lot of pain in a pregant woman's womb means that she will have a male child.
- If a pregnant woman dreams of death, she will have a miscarriage.
- If a pregnant woman goes out a lot at night, her baby will cry excessively.
- If you dream about flowers, someone you know is pregnant.
- A pregnant woman should never walk in the rain.
- If a pregnant woman eats while walking, she will have a difficult and painful delivery.
- If one dreams about mangos, a relative is pregnant.
- If a woman in her first pregnancy does not receive all of the best care, she will experience a difficult delivery.
- Acquiring anything for a baby before the birth might cause the unborn baby to die.
- It is shameful for a woman to show pain during a delivery.
- It will bring bad luck if a woman eats while holding an infant.
- If you have more than five long lines in your hand, you will have many children.
- It is bad manners to brag about the intelligence or ability of your children.
- A woman craving for green mangos, limes, or anything very sour means she is pregnant.
- A pregnant woman should never argue or be cross lest she give birth to a child who will be incorrigible.
- A child who gives you the most grief in life will be the one closest to you later in life.

(Ashby, 1983a, pp. 216–217)

special kind of food, the family must get that food. She was not to do any heavy work, especially during the early part of her pregnancy. She was not supposed to wash her clothes. She was supposed to rest, but not sleep too much; walk for a bit for exercise, but not too far and not under the rain and not while eating. She could also swim for exercise early in her pregnancy. One woman said she should not swim or bathe in the ocean, only in streams during pregnancy, but another woman said ocean swimming could be good exercise. Most important of all, the pregnant woman was supposed to be kept happy. She could take her walks, sing, and visit with family and friends, but she should not be allowed to be alone too long or to be unhappy.

Most societies have food-related beliefs and practices associated with menses, pregnancy, and lactation. As we see here and in later sections, Pohnpei is no exception. In Micronesian societies food-related beliefs and practices, especially those where the woman is provided with desired or special foods, including those that may be difficult to obtain, takes on special importance given the symbolic load that food carries. Providing such foods not only reinforces the social relations involved, but also tells the woman how important she is to the provider.

It's a Dangerous Time

People recognize that childbirth and the period surrounding it is a dangerous time and that sometimes women died. Throughout their pregnancy women were encouraged and helped to eat well and to take the proper local medicines so they would be strong enough to endure labor and delivery. One woman said, "If the uterus is healthy and strong, the delivery of a baby will be easy and have no serious problem. Otherwise, if it is unhealthy and weak, the mother will experience difficult delivery and serious problems."

Most of the "dos" of pregnancy have already been mentioned. The woman should be treated like a queen with her every whim fulfilled. She should engage in light exercise, such as walking and swimming, and other pleasurable activities. In addition, she should get up with the sun. She should have her stomach massaged regularly by a skilled person such as a local healer or a midwife. This massage has many purposes: to align the baby, to ease the delivery, to enhance general physical and psychological comfort, and to determine the sex of the child. Ashby (1983b) mentions that a pregnant woman should not eat while walking nor should she travel in a canoe without a cover on her, which would be consistent with the women's reports that women should not be directly exposed to the sun.

In Yasuo's report on "The Customs and Manners of Child-birth among the South Sea Islanders" he lists several things women in Pohnpei should not do while they are pregnant:

Activities which were absolutely forbidden include intercourse between the pregnant woman and her husband after the third month, moving about unclothed outside during daylight, going outside on rainy days or at

sunset, noon naps, touching the breasts, applying cosmetics, eating sea
anemones and eating too much sugar cane.

In addition the pregnant woman must never give rise to jealousy, speaking badly of and doing wrong to others is prohibited, and furthermore
small meals are prohibited and large meals are taken. (Yasuo, 1940, p. 4
of English language reprint)

Most of the "don'ts" reported during this study have already been
mentioned in the above paragraph or in earlier sections. The most commonly cited "don't" was that a pregnant woman should not eat while
she is walking, for if she did so she would have a prolonged labor with
"complicated pains." She was not to walk in the rain for similar reasons.
The pregnant woman should not sleep too much. She should not sleep
late into the morning and she should not sleep during the day. If she
did, she would have prolonged pain during labor or her child might be
born weak, or, as several women told us, she might actually "fall asleep
during labor" and not have a "good delivery." She should not expose
her breasts to the early sunrise or sunset, as this could affect her ability
to breast-feed. If she exposed her body to the sun at sunrise and sunset,
"her pains during labor would be very sharp and painful all over (scat-
tered pain throughout her womb)," like the rays of the sun. This is why
she was supposed to "get up with the sun" and bathe before the sun
was fully up. She should not bathe after sunset; in fact she should not
even be out of doors in the dark. If a woman bathed in a stream after
sunset a ghost might grab her and make her sick. One woman who was
not originally from the main island of Pohnpei told us that women who
were not from Pohnpei had to be particularly careful about bathing in
the streams after dark. This was because "the ghosts or bad spirits are
not friendly with strangers. If the spirits are not friendly with anyone,
they make the person get sick." The baby might also be affected if the
woman bathed after dark. It might be born with weak or deformed
bones.

The pregnant woman should not lift heavy things or strain herself.
She should avoid being alone, especially if she has to go out after sunset. She should avoid places known to be inhabited by spirits and she
(and those around her) should certainly avoid offending them. She
should keep busy and not allow herself to be sad. She should be especially careful to avoid any food traditionally taboo for her, but no other
specific foods have to be avoided.

Pregnant women were not supposed to wear leis during their pregnancy. If they did there could be a bad effect on the child when it is born.
For example, it might be born with the umbilical cord around its neck
and that might cause suffocation.

Seventh-Month Feast—*kamweng kasapw*

In the past the family would give the woman a feast (*kamweng kasapw* for Pohnpei or, according to Ashby [1983b], *sou* on Mokil) around the seventh month of pregnancy (see also Barnabas & Hezel, 1993). Ashby reports that on Pingelap there are "no formal celebrations or ceremonies" until after delivery (Ashby, 1983b, p. 31). The purpose of this feast, according to some of the women we interviewed, was to let the woman know she was important to the family and to give her the strength, perhaps more psychological and social than physical, to get through this potentially dangerous time. "The feast during pregnancy was to show appreciation and happiness that the lady is conceiving. She said that she doesn't believe that people are still practicing these important events. She believes that women are pregnant, and all we do is just wait until she is delivering; then we are happy."

Another woman told us, "They say they will have to make a party for her because they do not know after three months if she is returning or she will pass away. . . . And [to demonstrate] the family keep important to herself and she, herself, understand her position in the family, that she's something, that she is important to them."

This explanation is similar to the one offered by Ashby, although none of the women mentioned visiting her parents for the feast. "After six or seven months of pregnancy, the woman and her husband visit her parents for a feast called *kamweng kasapw*. On this occasion, half of the foods are donated by both the wife's and the husband's families. Historically *kamweng kasapw* was a farewell feast for an expectant mother in case she did not survive the birth of her child" (Ashby, 1983a, p. 188; 1983b, p. 27).

The women's descriptions add elements not found in the material by Ashby. The women point out that the feast was not just a farewell feast, but also celebrated the pregnancy, and, perhaps more importantly given the potential danger of childbirth, it reminded the mother-to-be and both families that she was important and had an important position in the family. It also brought both families together to further cement their relationship. Barnabas and Hezel (1993) suggest that this feast is less common today, that in fact it has "virtually died out, since modern medical care has rendered the survival of the mother and child far less doubtful than in former days" (Barnabas & Hezel, 1993, pp. 11–12).

Determining the Sex of the Unborn Child

Several women reported that certain women in the community were especially good at determining the sex of the unborn child (see also M.C.

Ward, 1989). One of the techniques involved massage of the abdomen. According to one woman, this special skill was often passed from mother to daughter.

Yasuo (1940) suggests the following technique could be used in Pohnpei: "The milk of the pregnant woman is dropped into water, and if this coagulates it will be a boy, and if not a girl will be born. In addition it is said that a foetus on the left side of the abdomen will be a girl and one on the right a boy" (Yasuo, 1940, p. 7 of English language reprint).

Time to Leave School

Although this may be changing, a girl is expected to leave school if she gets pregnant. One woman who left school shortly before she graduated talked at some length about her regret at not having completed her education. Toward the end of the interview, when she was asked whether she had anything she wanted to add or whether there was something she wanted young people to know, this is what she talked about. She wanted us to encourage young girls to wait until they finished school to get pregnant or to go back to school after the baby was born. She said they needed to realize that they were decreasing their opportunities, that the lack of education would prevent them from getting some of the better jobs in the community. This seemed to be the general sentiment among the women.

In an informal interview with a woman in her early to mid-20s I asked if young women were ever sad or depressed after they gave birth. She told me that the ones who have to give up school get depressed. They want to go back to school and to do things with their friends, but they have to stay home and take care of the baby. She told me of a friend in that situation. Every time the friend went off to spend some time with friends, leaving the baby in her mother's or someone else's care, the mother kept calling her to come home to take care of her baby. This would upset the girl, and she would talk to her friend about how unhappy she was now; she wanted to go back to school but she could not because she had a child to care for.

The option of going back to school after childbirth, or even at a later date, seems relatively new. In the past, according to some, pregnancy marked the end of a young woman's education. In fact, some who did not like school may have used pregnancy as a way out. Today, when young women want to go back to school there may be some difficulty. We were told, as in the story above, that many parents expect the new mother to stay home and take care of the baby; they expect her to assume the responsibilities of parenthood. Although adoption or foster-age (see Chapter 6), formal or informal, within the family might have been an option in the past for a girl not yet ready to assume an adult role, this is often not the case today. Grandparents and potential adoptive parents may be working or, according to some, they may simply not want to take on the care or economic burden of a young child again.

Local Medicine

As noted earlier, women in the past often regularly consumed an herbal preparation designed to help them cleanse their bodies and maintain their health. Similar, if not the same, preparations could be used during pregnancy for the same reasons. Again, as noted earlier, one woman suggested these preparations probably provided additional vitamins, like the vitamin supplements of today. Several of the older women suggested that young people today are not as healthy as they were and are even in older age, because young people do not regularly use local medicines. They also linked the discontinued regular use of local medicine to health problems, such as cancer, among older women.

> We asked them if there were local medicines that they take during pregnancies. They said they used to drink a lot of local medicines. They believed that it helped to keep them strong and healthy. They believe that because young mothers do not practice taking these local medicines they are weak and unhealthy. They believe that because they used to drink these local medicines a lot during pregnancies, their cervix were clean. Nowadays, we have uterus cancer because we do not drink these local medicines for cleaning of the cervix before and after birth.

The women told us that a variety of herbal preparations could be used during pregnancy. According to one woman, one of the herbal preparations used in the past during pregnancy was said to keep the baby cool while it also cooled the inside of the uterus. Ashby reports that a medicine made from the squeezed leaves of the *tehn likoahmw* vine was used because it was "cooling to the stomach" (Ashby, 1983b, p. 27).

This was the only time that any of the women (or the literature) mentioned something that seemed to be related to something like a hot/cold theory of health and illness. In this case it appears that some women consider pregnancy as symbolically hot so the woman needs to take something cool to bring the temperature of her uterus and the baby into proper balance. This woman also said there was an herbal drink "to cool inside the urinal part when sometimes it feels burning when infected."

We were told that "everybody knows about these medicines" or at least they did when these women were having their babies.

Another woman told us "that they also have local medicine to make the head of the baby smaller during delivery. Although it tasted awful, she took it because she believed it would help her. Same with the medicines she took to help her to have easy delivery of the babies."

In the past, and often even today, women may visit a local healer or midwife during their pregnancy (see also M.C. Ward, 1989, and R.L. Ward, 1977). One reason they go is for regular massage. This massage is viewed as both comforting and relaxing for the mother, but it also is used to determine whether the baby is in a good position and if not, then to manipulate it into a better position. Some of these healers, nearly all of whom are women, are known to be especially good at predicting the gender of the baby.

Pregnancy-Related "Sicknesses"

R.L. Ward (1977) notes that although it is not strictly a sickness, pregnancy was viewed as associated with uncomfortable or unpleasant feelings commonly linked with sickness, such as vomiting, backache, and sore breasts. Pregnant women were also viewed as particularly vulnerable during this time; thus they needed to be protected and kept happy.

Morning Sickness

As already noted, feeling sick and throwing up all the time (commonly known as morning sickness) was viewed as one of the core signs of pregnancy, even among those few women who reported they had never experienced it. However, far more women reported experiencing morning sickness than did not. Things like certain smells exacerbated morning sickness for some women. There were other, seemingly bizarre things that could also cause a bout of nausea and vomiting. "This lady said she could tell [she was pregnant] by not wanting to eat anymore. The first time she got pregnant, she took her ring from her finger that her father gave her and threw it away. Every time she looked at the ring, she would throw up. She didn't know why, but she just didn't like it on her finger anymore."

Another woman told us that a certain song always made her feel ill. "My husband and his friends used to sit outside our window and sing this song. I called to them to stop singing that song. I didn't like it. But they kept singing that song and I kept getting sick. Even now I don't like to hear that song."

Women offered little in terms of remedies to control morning sickness, although apparently there were some local medicines that could be used. Several women said that during this time many of them ate sour fruits. Not only did they crave such fruits, but also these fruits seemed to be one of the few foods that did not make them feel sicker.

Spirit or Ghost Sickness—soumwauen eni

Women rarely talked about sicknesses during pregnancy or in the post-partum period even though they were specifically asked if there were any illnesses associated with these times. More often women talked in terms of prevention, like not walking alone or bathing in the dark. The purpose of these practices was to avoid encounters with or possession by spirits. A couple of women talked more specifically about sicknesses from the ghosts or spirits, *soumwauen eni*, in particular sickness from the sea ghosts, *soumwauen naniak*. Hezel (personal communication, July 1999) notes that "the fear of malevolent spirits during pregnancy and after childbirth is standard throughout Micronesia. The most vulnerable class of people was women around the time of childbirth, it seems." It was clear, however, that it is difficult to distinguish the "normal" signs and symptoms of pregnancy from those associated with spirit sicknesses.

One woman was asked, "How could people tell that someone was sick from the evil spirits?" The woman responded (translated summary):

The signs of a mother being sick from the evil spirit are being fussy, always grumpy, short temper, and sometimes sad. This explains when a mother is unhappy and tends to silently sit or lay by herself quietly. When someone talks to her, she would either respond with one word only or not at all with clipped lips. She may even be crying silently without any sound. When annoyed, she would either yell out her response to a question or not answer at all. Sometimes she would be too sick and start to feel nauseated, vomiting, and always feeling upset. She even feels she would like to be left alone by herself.

Dr. Maureen asked whether these are symptoms of pregnancy or whether these are the signs of sickness after birth.

She said that these are the symptoms of a sick mother who is suffering from the evil spirits. When a pregnant woman or a mother with new infant is demonstrating these symptoms, they always believed that she is sick by the evil spirits, so then they start to find medicines or find someone to fix medicine for her if they do not know how to do it themselves.

However these symptoms may seem similar to those of a pregnant woman, the families don't ignore the possibility that there might be some evil spirit sickness associated with it. For instance, if the pregnant woman is showing those symptoms of evil spirit sickness, but the family doesn't try to cure it before she delivers her baby, when she gives birth to the baby, her sickness will be worse, or both of them might be sick.

Therefore, the family will try to find cures for her sickness during the pregnancy period, in order to avoid any prolonged side effects which might get worse during delivery. They used to believe that if she (the pregnant woman) is not cured, Satan will eventually possess the baby once it is born, and that will make the baby sick also. . .

In order to drive away the evil spirits, there is a special way to apply the medicinal herb. Someone among the women (local healers) would chew the herb and spread it all over the body of the sick woman by blowing out the chewed herbs all over her. This term is called *purak*.

There are, of course, other curative procedures and remedies. One of the younger women reported that she "did go to one lady and she massaged my stomach, when I was four months pregnant, because I had cramps all over. I thought I was going to give birth that day. And when I went there they said that the placenta was below the fetus. That's what they found."

The treatment did not work and she continued to have cramps. In her eighth month her family gave her local medicine to drink. "They said it was good for *soumwauen naniak*. . . . Before they gave me, before they gave me the medication I was feeling bad. Like I was really weak, my stomach. And after that, after they gave me my medication I believe that I felt much better than before. Yeah, it was like my body was relieved from something."

The descriptions of spirit or ghost sickness offered by the women in this study focused on uncomfortable feelings states (symptoms) and different or unusual, even asocial, behaviors (signs). None of their descriptions involved altered states of consciousness or anything that might be appropriately described as possession. However, information on possession in Micronesia, including Chuuk and Pohnpei, presented by Dobbin and Hezel (e.g., 1996; Hezel, 1994b) suggest that possession might also be possible. They have noted that in recent years possession is more often associated with women than with men, and that it can occur during pregnancy and times of social crisis. Hezel (personal communication, July 1999) notes that in the work with Dobbin, only a couple of instances of possession occurred before delivery, and these were connected to some problem. "In a couple of cases, girls who were being reproached for becoming pregnant before marriage went into trance states, thus speaking their piece on the matter while 'blaming' some dead family member for the intervention." This social/psychological use of possession states, with or without an altered state of consciousness, is common in the literature on possession and trance; people use such opportunities to air grievances or to manipulate their worlds and relationships, especially where they commonly have little power (e.g., Bourguignon, 1976; Fitzgerald, 1983; Walker, 1972; AvRuskin, 1988). Possession, which involves trance behavior interpreted as the result of possession by a spirit, may be another form of spirit sickness, although possession is not necessarily viewed as illness in Pohnpei.

"Feeling Bad Sickness"—soumwau en insensued

Fidelity, or more precisely, worry about fidelity, appears to be a significant Pohnpeian cultural theme. Such worries, according to R.L. Ward (1977), could potentially lead to illness, something he reports as "feeling bad sickness" or *soumwau en insensued* (see also Chapter 6). Although the women did not specifically talk about this "feeling bad sickness," their comments made it quite clear that worry about the husband's fidelity could result in the pregnant woman or a new mother becoming quite distressed, even ill.

> Emotional upset caused by grief over the death of a close relative or by the knowledge that one's spouse is having an affair is *soumwau en insensued* "feeling bad sickness." Bad feelings are regarded as a sickness only if the unhappiness persists over a period of time and is manifested as chronic depression, withdrawal, or in terms of one or more of the following symptoms: constriction of the throat muscles and difficulty swallowing; the feeling that something is welling up and is stuck in the throat; a small, continuous cough; a feeling of emptiness in the stomach even after one has eaten; confused and disconnected conversation; a preoccupation with thoughts of the departed relative or lover and repeated references to that person; and a failure to take note of present events and company. Other physical symptoms are pain at the crown of the head and at the points just above the eyes where the nose meets the forehead. (R.L. Ward, 1977, p. 79)

Concern about a husband's fidelity was apparently quite common and perhaps with some basis, considering the expected period of sexual abstinence. The couple was expected to abstain from sex from the time they became aware of the pregnancy to anywhere from one month to several years after the birth of the child.

R.L. Ward (1977) notes that "feeling bad" during pregnancy is dangerous for both the mother and the fetus. The "bad blood" that results from anger and anxiety can pass from the woman to the unborn child. This can result in a miscarriage or the baby being born "crossed-eyed, ugly, or retarded" (R.L. Ward, 1977, p. 80).

Sickness of the Baby

To avoid illness or problems with the newborn, the family and the mother bear responsibility for proper behavior during pregnancy and the postpartum period. In the past, this responsibility arose primarily from traditional beliefs. Today it often comes primarily from the teachings of the hospital and clinic staff and is based on ideas from biomedicine. Thus, especially in the past, if the family did not make sure a mother was kept happy and ate and lived well during her pregnancy (treated like a queen), the result could be a child who was sick or impaired. If the mother did not take good care of herself during pregnancy, this could also cause the baby to be born sickly or with a physical impairment. One woman reported that "the term they used when the mother is careless during pregnancy is *wia kaw*."

Today, through antenatal visits, posters, and fliers from the Health Department and the popular media, pregnant women receive varying amounts and kinds of information on the potential effects of their behavior (e.g., diet, exercise, use of drugs and alcohol, etc.) during pregnancy. The message is, again, that certain kinds of behaviors during this period can affect the unborn child. The emphasis is, however, more often on the pregnant woman's behavior rather than that of her family. Support from the family is still viewed as important, but the emphasis has shifted somewhat.

NOTES

1. Hezel (personal communication, July 1999) makes a distinction between adoption and fosterage (see the section on adoption in Chapter 6).

2. Menstrual cycles for the first couple of years after menarche are often anovulatory (no egg is produced). The result is that during this time young women are generally infertile. This is often referred to in the medical literature as adolescent sterility.

3. The two collaborators on the project suggested there might be a relationship with the period of building and roadworks associated with establishing the seat of the national government at Palikir, which occurred about the same time. There are reports in the literature from across the Pacific of young women using sexual favors to gain access to valued goods, so this explanation is within the realm of possibility (see for example, Falgout, 1993 for Pohnpei).

Chapter 5

Birthing—*neitik*

One of the oldest women told us this story to explain why women now deliver babies vaginally.

She says that, before, they were only able to deliver the first child because they never realized that the baby had to come naturally out of the opening. So what they did was they cut the womb of the mother and take out the baby and if the mother survived she's lucky. But most of the mothers died even at the first born. 'Cause even the dissecting, because I know that they take a piece of the shell, they use the seashell. Very sharp but still it is not that thin. A certain shell they used to just cut down the womb and take out the babies and then the babies and the mothers they don't always survive. But later they said a couple, the lady was pregnant, and this couple went out sitting by the seashore. And this stingray came to the shore to deliver. And maybe the stingray was trying to deliver the baby right in front of them. So they were just watching and the baby just came out naturally through that hole. When they saw that they said: "Oh so maybe we can go try this. Maybe we will just let the baby come out from the hole down there." So that's when the first couple went and said OK, when the time comes we just wait if the baby will come out just like what happened with the stingray. And since then that is what has been happening.

The majority of deliveries today are vaginal deliveries. One informant at the hospital told me that they have about one C-section (Caesarean delivery, a delivery via incision of the abdominal wall and uterus) per month. They are generally associated with complications of pregnancy, such as placenta previa. Only one of the women involved in the formal interviews reported having delivered by C-section.

DELIVERY PLACE

One of the oldest women told us that only her first child was born at the hospital. She delivered all the rest at home. She preferred the home deliveries because her mother and her aunts could be with her. They could not only give her support and assist with the delivery, but could also provide the necessary local medicines.

The other woman present during this interview told a story about one of her deliveries at home. In this story, which she told with much humor, she "cussed" at her aunts. They were supposed to take care of her and she was messy and bloody and wanted to be cleaned up, so she yelled at them. They told her she needed to treat them better or they would go away and leave her all alone.

Other older women delivered all their babies at home. One woman told us that her older sister assisted with the delivery of her first two children, but that she delivered all of the rest alone in her own home.

> Even her husband usually went out either to farm or somewhere else so that he always missed when the babies were delivered. By the time he got home he would hear the cry of the baby already born. She would deliver each of them by herself, and when the baby is out, she would cut the cord herself and clean herself and the baby and wait for the family members to come home. The father would be surprised to come home and hear the cry of a newborn.
>
> On the very next day, she is already up and strong to wash her own dirty clothes. She would only leave the rest of the family members' clothes for her sisters to help her with. But her own dirty clothes and her baby's clothes would be washed by herself.

This woman and another who had all of her babies at home did not have mothers available to them at the time their children were born. In one case the woman's mother had died when she was a small child; in the other case, the woman's mother was very old and unable to help when she began to have children.

It is not clear whether women who gave birth at "home" did so in a separate structure, in the bush or jungle, or in a section of the family's usual dwelling. We have reports of all three. For example, in one story the woman talks about giving birth in the "jungle." Several women report that home births occurred in the home of the woman, her mother, or her mother-in-law. Like Yasuo (1940), one woman, reported that births generally took place in a specially built structure. "After the sixth month the expectant mother erects a birth hut on the shore thatched with coconut leaves where she resides with her husband's mother, or else returned to her parents' house and lives with her family" (Yasuo, 1940, p. 4 of English language reprint).

Yasuo also says:

> The delivery occurs within an unfrequented coconut grove or inside a room, but recently delivery in the forest has diminished. The expectant mother chooses the place in the forest, but the birth hut is for the most part newly constructed on the seashore and is built in such a manner that it can not be seen into from the outside. (Yasuo, 1940, p. 8 of English language reprint)

Yasuo's report suggests his data were collected in terms of coastal dwellers. Because a significant portion of the population in Pohnpei lives in the interior, it is very possible that the site of the actual birth might have varied according to the specific circumstances and was not something that followed any regular rule.

When women gave birth at "home" they could engage in any of the traditional beliefs and practices they wished or that their family insisted upon. But today, according to some women, when people go to the hospital they leave all the traditions behind. One woman said, "They don't let, they don't allow it." Discussions with people knowledgeable about the hospital's practices and some hospital staff confirm that the hospital discourages many traditional practices, particularly those that involve local medicines. If more than one woman is in labor in the small, tightly packed, one-room labor unit, family members may not be allowed to stay because it could make the other woman or women uncomfortable. These women would not want others to witness any "faces" or sounds they might make. This would cause the woman and her family great shame.

By the late 1980s more than 90% of all births in Pohnpei took place in the hospital, with the majority attended by a nurse or midwife (Government of the Federated States of Micronesia, 1990). Information collected as part of this project suggests that the birth experience of women in Pohnpei today bears little resemblance to the experiences of women in the past who more often gave birth at home. In many ways, women have left their traditions behind to give birth in the hospital. In talking about hospital births, the word *tradition* seems to be more related to the customs of the hospital and Western biomedicine than to the historical traditions and customs of this particular society. The typical birth experience of today is a "traditional" hospital birth, one that follows the needs and customs of the hospital and the beliefs of many Western-trained hospital staff rather than the historical traditions and customs of Pohnpei and the cultures represented in Pohnpeian society today. The birthing experience in Pohnpei today seems to have lost much of its unique flavor and probably has more in common with hospital births in other countries throughout the world than with the experiences of these women's ancestors.

Some of the women, particularly some of the younger women, report that they prefer giving birth in the hospital and are happy that the rules do not allow family members or, even more importantly, nonfamily to be present during labor and delivery. These women say they want to be alone or to have only hospital personnel present; they do not want anyone to see or hear them because they might behave badly and bring shame to their family (see below).

BELIEFS AND PRACTICES ASSOCIATED WITH BIRTHING

Particularly in the past, childbirth was considered a very dangerous time for both the mother and her baby. The first delivery was of particular concern because the young woman had not yet demonstrated that she could survive this dangerous and life-threatening event. As noted earlier, sometime between the seventh and the ninth month the first-time mother might be given a feast. This feast showed the woman and the community that she was loved, but it was also a farewell feast in case she did not survive childbirth.

Avoiding Problems during Delivery

As already noted above, many of the practices during pregnancy were associated with avoiding problems and ensuring that the woman had an easy delivery. In addition to the practices already mentioned, it was important to resolve any bad feelings toward the family of the pregnant woman before she went into labor. If they were not resolved, the woman could have a difficult delivery and might even die. Hard feelings or problems within the family also needed to be resolved so the baby would be born into a happy family.

Yasuo (1940) reports that as the time of delivery approached, an experienced midwife was asked to pray for a safe delivery. He also suggests that items such as pigs, fish, and fruit were offered to the spirits of the ancestors to help assure a safe delivery. None of the women specifically talked about the use of prayer or spirit offerings, but it was clear that midwives used a variety of techniques and that prayer is an integral part of all aspects of people's lives. So it is likely both were involved in the past, if not today.

All You Can Hear Is the Baby Cry: Behavior during Birthing

One doctor told me: "You should go and walk by the labor and delivery room at the hospital. You wouldn't believe it. You will be surprised. It is so quiet. All you can hear is the baby cry." All the women interviewed told us that Pohnpeian women do not cry out during childbirth. The only sound is the baby's cry when it is born.

These women told us that for Pohnpeian women it is a sign of honor not to cry or make a noise during labor and delivery; other women may cry out but not Pohnpeian women—or those involved in Pohnpeian families. If a Pohnpeian woman cries out it will bring great shame to the family. "Oh, it's a shame [to cry out]! If you start making faces, they say, listen don't do that, people will think you are a coward. You can have the baby. Now you have to show the face as when you created the baby. [Everyone laughs.] Yeah, they saying things, you know."

Even though all the women in the room broke into loud laughter at this comment, every one of them agreed with it, and we heard similar comments on other occasions. Clearly the reference is to the faces a woman makes during sex with the suggestion that women make the same kind of faces during birthing. Furthermore, women are supposed to have enjoyed "making the baby" so they should not complain when they have to deal with the consequences of that act.

Most discussions about why women do not make noise focus on it as a sign of honor and Pohnpeian women's strength and pride. Others told us that at least in the past, women did not cry out because they did not want anyone outside the family, or the men in the family, to know they were giving birth. If others heard the mother's cries and knew she was giving birth, they might worry unduly, or perhaps more importantly, someone who did not like the mother or her family, clan, or lineage, or had some quarrel with them, might evoke a spell that would prolong the mother's labor or even cause her death or that of the child.

One woman told us that it was important, however, to notify all the key women in the family, that they should all be invited to be in attendance. If the woman's labor seemed prolonged, those gathered considered, among other things, whether they may have missed informing someone important and whether this person, perhaps unintentionally, was prolonging the labor. "One time this woman was in labor a long time. They thought about who they had not told. Someone remembered an auntie had not been told. Someone went and told the auntie. When she arrived, the baby was born. They told her see it was you that was holding the baby back because you thought we did not want to tell you."

Most women told us that when women give birth at home everyone except specific women are sent away from the house. This is so they cannot hear the woman if she should cry out. There was one exception, however: one woman from one of the outer islands told us that the husband would be present, that he would sit behind the mother to support her while she gave birth. This was so she could have someone strong to push against.

One woman involved in an informal interview took this "no one will hear me scream" issue to the extreme and went off by herself to have her baby.

> She had gone out fishing and when she came back she went to bathe. As she was returning from her bath she started to have cramps. She knew it was just about time and she wanted to hide so no one would know. She went into the jungle and laid out some leaves under a tree, "just like a pig getting ready to give birth." Then she sat down and tried to have her baby.
>
> But, it turns out, she was not alone. Her sister and mother had been watching her closely, as they knew her time was getting close. The sister followed her into the jungle and hid and watched her sister. When she knew that her sister really was close to giving birth she went and told their mother. The mother came to be with her and sent a son down to get the old midwife. Her mother was very nervous; she did not want her to have the baby before the midwife came. She did not know what to do and ran around all excited, telling her daughter to wait. "Cross your legs or something. Don't have it yet."
>
> The brother had to carry the old midwife up the hill on his back. She was very old and could no longer walk. She had one droopy eye. She was very old. As soon as she arrived the mother calmed down and the baby was born soon after. However, the baby was born with the cord around its neck. The baby nearly died. The old woman took the cord off the baby's neck and declared this would be "a struggling child," the child had struggled in the womb and would continue to struggle throughout its life. (Excerpt from field notes)

Ashby also notes that women do not cry out during labor or delivery. "It is considered quite shameful for the expectant mother to show pain by crying out during labor or the actual birth. Consequently, the woman's relatives are usually present during the delivery as an incentive to silence. To show great pain to outsiders is especially painful" (Ashby, 1983a, p. 188).

Female relatives were present for more than an incentive to not cry out: they also provided considerable support and made the woman feel loved and cared for.

I Want My Mother

All the women said they wanted their mothers with them for the birth (or at least the first birth) and for a time afterward. Most felt that women in general would want their mothers with them. In the past, if the woman did not already live with her mother then the woman often traveled to her mother's house to have her baby in the mother's home or the nearby hospital. Other women would stay in their husband's home, but the mother would come to stay with her for at least a week and perhaps a month or more. According to Demory (1976), mothers did not stay long because it could be difficult to have two mothers (the woman's mother and her mother-in-law) in the same household.

There was divided opinion about whether or not mothers-in-law would have been, or should be, present for the birth. Some said the mother-in-law would be there; others said it generally depended on the relationship between the mother-in-law and the woman. At least one woman indicated that after the birth of her first child she wanted her mother-in-law rather than her mother in attendance. This woman seemed to feel especially close to her mother-in-law, with whom she lived. Her mother-in-law was also especially knowledgeable about women's health issues and may have been a local healer. Other women made it quite clear they did not want their mothers-in-law there, that if the mother-in-law did not like the woman she might not be supportive, that she might even be critical of her daughter-in-law's behavior, that daughters-in-law would feel shame in front of their mothers-in-law. When asked if a woman's mother-in-law should be present during the birth, one woman put it this way: "I don't know. I feel uncomfortable having my mother-in-law beside me when I am in labor, because I do not know her heart to me. So I try to have my own mother and my grandmother to keep closer, and my sister, but on the part of the man I don't know."

This woman's comment is consistent with a comment made by R.L. Ward: "An expectant mother residing with her husband's family may return to her own family to bear a child, fearing possible sorcery from her mother-in-law or sister-in-law" (R.L. Ward, 1977, pp. 213–214).

Although some suggest that relationships between a woman and her female in-laws are generally strong and supportive (see also Kihleng, 1996), others suggest there is often a regular and persistent tension between these women (see also Demory, 1976; R.L. Ward, 1977).

Most women indicated that in the past other women were likely to be present during a birth. This could include a traditional midwife or local healer and older aunties. However, these women were expected to stay at the woman's head. Only the mother and the midwife or healer could be positioned facing the mother.

Most women said that younger females, especially those who had not yet given birth, would not be in attendance; they might not even know the woman was in labor. As noted above, they too were sent away during the birth.

According to one woman, in the past, a traditional midwife was the primary attendant during the woman's pregnancy, delivery, and for several months after the birth. The way she described it, the midwife acted very much like a personal care attendant in the period surrounding childbirth. Although others certainly spoke of midwives or traditional birth attendants in regard to this period of time, only this woman emphasized her presence. I wondered what would happen if more than one woman in the area was pregnant. She suggested that it would be unusual for more than one woman to be pregnant at a time, that the population was much smaller in the past, but that even if that occurred, there were always several midwives available.

If no one else is in labor in the Pohnpei hospital, a woman can have her mother and other female kin near her during labor, although not during delivery. During the birth the family must wait outside.

One doctor was asked why this was so. He said it was "tradition," but by that he meant hospital tradition, not Pohnpeian tradition. His comments and that of others suggest that the hospital staff see family members as being "in the way." The delivery room in Pohnpei is small, but not so small as to preclude the presence of additional people. We were told that the delivery room in Chuuk is so small that there simply isn't enough room for anyone but the hospital staff to be in attendance. One person also suggested that the presence of additional people increased the risk of infection or the breaking of sterile fields.

In the 1970s Demory (1976, p. 61) reported that "mothers are allowed to attend their daughters through labor and delivery in the obstetrics unit." However, according to one of our informants from the Health Department others are not allowed in the labor room because they make the woman uncomfortable: she does not want anyone to see her if she behaves in a shameful way.

According to this informant, some doctors are beginning to allow family members in the delivery room. Some of the staff disapprove of this practice. Others suggest the hospital simply does not have enough gowns to routinely allow family members in the delivery room. They also note that the labor and delivery unit is too small to allow many people to be present. For some the sentiment seems to be "this is, after all, Pohnpei, not the U.S." The implied message seemed to be that women in places such as the United States are too pampered during labor and delivery, that they are not tough and proud like Pohnpeian women.

A few women suggested that mothers should be allowed to be with their daughters during the delivery. A couple of other women said they would have liked their husbands with them. One day when I raised this issue with one of the clinic doctors, he posed this question to a pregnant woman: "Who would you like with you in the delivery room?" "Nobody. I want to be alone." "What if you had to choose between your mother or your husband—which would you choose?" When she answered "my mother" it was quite clear that she did not want her husband there. Thus, although many older women indicated that they thought someone from the family should be allowed to be with the woman during childbirth, some may not want a change in the status quo.

Nevertheless, considering the general movement in other countries toward more homelike hospital and clinic births, situations where the woman can choose to have others present and choose her birthing position, Pohnpeians may need to consider alternative birthing options for hospital or clinic-based births. Like women in other countries, some of the older women thought that the presence of mothers, and possibly husbands, might be a healthier and more supportive birth context; on the other hand, many young women have no experience with such contexts and may be reluctant to consider other options.

If at some time in the future hospital practices change in regards to labor and delivery, the issues raised here should be kept in mind. It will be necessary to have a labor and delivery unit where women can have privacy (with or without family members) if they so desire. This appears to be a critical issue for all the women with whom we talked. These women do not want anyone outside of the family (or hospital staff) to know how they behave during labor and delivery, and they want to be kept safe from any bad feelings and the dangerous implications of bad feelings.

Local Medicine

Several women told us that around the time of delivery, women drank *sakau* (kava) to "cleanse" the baby and to make the delivery easier.[1] One woman totally disagreed. She was adamant that Pohnpeian women never touched *sakau*, that she had been told by some very old women, "wise in the culture," that this was not true. She said that women who said such things were reinventing Pohnpeian culture to meet some need of their own.

A few weeks later we had the opportunity to ask the opinion of an older woman from that same municipality.

> We asked if it is true that women in the past never drank the Pohnpeian *sakau*, but she said it is not true. She believes that women already started drinking the *sakau* with the men even before she was born because as she grew older she used to see them drinking, and it seemed to be something acceptable. She was born in 1927, and she believes that women might have started drinking with the men even before the 1900s. She said that she also heard of that story that women never drank the kava, but she imagined it could have been long, long time ago, before 1900. She said that for those years it is hard to find someone to attest to this story, however. She can only speak of what she knew that actually happened during her time. So she said that people talked about women drinking *sakau*. However, no one who might have witnessed it is alive to say that it was true. She can only attest that women already drank with the men as far back as the early 1900s.

We also asked this woman why women would drink *sakau* during pregnancy:

> She said that it is to clean the "white stuff," like mucous, all over the baby when it's born. If the mother drinks the *sakau* during pregnancy, the baby will be clean when born. *Mehmehnuht kilin seri*, or powderlike skin, is what they called the body of the baby when it is born with the white stuff all over it. The people during her time used to believe that the body would have a hard time coming out of the mother's womb if it is covered with that "white stuff." If it is clean, it would be easily delivered.

There were, however, other local medicines that could be used. Generally these were special medicines known to midwives and other health specialists. Many of these were herbal preparations, which were either ingested or rubbed on the woman's body, but others involved chants or prayers. They were used to assist with difficult deliveries, especially prolonged labor.

When there was a prolonged labor the women would begin to think about why this might be so. They would review the woman's behavior and that of her family during her pregnancy. They would consider whether there were any family problems or hard feelings between the woman's family and any others. They would also think about whether all the appropriate women had been told that labor had begun. If they unintentionally forgot to tell a woman, she might, again unintentionally, cause the labor to be prolonged. As already noted, in one story the women forgot to tell one of the aunties the woman was in labor. The baby was born soon after the auntie arrived. If troubles within the family were deemed to be the problem, if possible, the family would be brought together to resolve those problems. If they thought it could be a curse or spell, they asked the healer to use the necessary medicines or alternative spells. This could be dangerous, however, because the spell could come back to the healer if the counterspell was not correct or the other spell was too strong. It was better to make amends with any offended person or family, preferably well before the woman went into labor, and then it was important to keep the fact that she was in labor hidden until the child was born and all was well with her and the child.

The hospital staff discourages the use of local medicines, especially at the time of delivery. One way this is done is making the women "NPO" (nothing per os or nothing by mouth) during labor. According to one informant, local medicines contain an ingredient similar to pitocin that enhances contractions. If women take the local medicine too soon or take too much, it can result in fetal distress, and one sign of this distress is the presence of meconium stool (dark, tarry feces). Of particular concern is the inability to regulate the amount of the labor-enhancing drug. Thus the hospital staff prefer to have the woman free of local medicines so they can use methods such as a pitocin drip to regulate contractions.

This does not mean that women today never use local medicines during a hospital delivery. If the use of local medicines is really important to the woman or her family, they will often find a way. What this means is that women either take the medicines before they go to the hospital, which is often early in labor, or have it brought to them at the hospital. Such interventions are more likely to happen, it seems, if there appears to be complications or if people think that the labor is longer than normal. One woman told a story that happened a few years ago in another FSM state. It involves a niece who was having a prolonged labor. Such things also happen, at least occasionally, in Pohnpei.

> My niece was in the hospital to have her baby. It was "taking too long for the baby to come out." The family decides that they should seek the help of a woman with traditional knowledge about these things. One of the best they knew was a relative. She happened to be at the hospital sitting with a grandchild. So they had one of the family sit with the child

and she and others from the family sneaked out in the early hours of the morning to collect the necessary herbs so the woman could make the preparation.

In those days no one was allowed to stay with a woman in labor, so the girl was all alone. No mother, no husband like in American hospitals. So they went to the windows to get the girl's attention. She was just walking up and down. They told her to come outside, as they had something that might help her. Other members of the family went down the hall to be sure the staff was kept diverted.

The girl went outside with the older woman and the woman rubbed the ointment all over her body. Then she went back inside. Not too long later she finally delivered a healthy baby. The family is convinced that the ointment helped, that the ointment helped to speed things up. (Field note summary of nontape-recorded interview)

Birthing Position

Most of the women we asked told us that in the past women often gave birth in a sitting or semireclining position. A woman, or according to one woman the husband, sat behind the woman to give her support, something to push against. In one interview it was mentioned that a woman could give birth standing but that this was considered potentially dangerous for the baby. The sense was that women in the past had some say about the birthing position. Today women generally give birth in the hospital and apparently conform to the hospital's expectation and deliver lying on a standard delivery table. As noted earlier, one doctor described hospital deliveries as following "tradition"—hospital tradition.

MISCARRIAGE

The women did not really say very much about miscarriages. They were mentioned, particularly in the context of obtaining pregnancy histories, but they were not discussed in any great detail. Miscarriages happened sometimes and for some women quite often. Clearly miscarriages indicated that something was wrong, but with one exception, the women did not really elaborate on this.

The one woman who talked about a miscarriage was quite distressed by it. The miscarriage happened during her first marriage, the only one of her three marriages in which she was very much in love. Her mother, however, did not approve of the young man and tried to break up the marriage. The young woman generally had irregular periods, so when she missed a couple of months she was not concerned. Then she began to bleed. She thought it was just her period, but her mother told her she was having a miscarriage and took her to the hospital. She was very sad when she learned that she had miscarried. She had very much wanted a child with this husband. She tried to get pregnant again, but when it seemed that it was not going to happen, she adopted two children. She was sure she would get pregnant once she adopted children. She did not get pregnant and her mother eventually managed to break up her marriage. Subsequently, her mother chose new husbands for her. She did not like these men, even though the men and their families were generally good to her. She kept running away from the men and going to her mother's house. Her mother would yell at her and then try to arrange another marriage. The young woman did not want these men, she still wanted her first husband, but by this time he had remarried. During these additional marriages she hoped that at least she would get pregnant, but it never happened. She seemed certain now that she lost the first baby, never got pregnant again, and was unable to develop a caring relationship with new husbands because something was wrong with her, that somehow she was unworthy of her own child and a happy marriage. At least some of this belief appeared to be situated within a difficult relationship between the woman and her mother. The younger woman thought she was not being a good daughter because she disagreed with her mother on some issues, such as whom who she should marry. Because she was not a good daughter, she thought, she was punished with a miscarriage and childlessness and a general, nearly all-encompassing feeling of sadness. Thus, in this woman's case, the miscarriage and her inability to conceive were tied to beliefs associated with problems in a core interpersonal relationship, one we discussed at some length.

R.L. Ward (1977) writes that people believed a miscarriage could result from an affair with a male demon or spirit from the land, the mangrove swamp, or the sea. Such an affair could occur without the woman realizing that she had had sex with someone other than her husband. The result of the affair is a "spirit pregnancy or *liseian en ni*" (R.L. Ward, 1977, p. 85). According to Ward, the "culprit spirit is often Nahnsau, and the medicine used by some curers is for mangrove sickness. Hence it is not clear whether 'spirit pregnancy' should be regarded as a subcategory of mangrove sickness" (R.L. Ward, 1977, p. 85).

BIRTHRATES

Among the oldest women interviewed and reports from others about women in the oldest age groups, the total number of pregnancies among women in the 60-plus age group was often in the double digits (e.g., 12 to 20); reports of 16 and 18 pregnancies were common. In many cases most of these children survived infancy and early childhood. One woman reported that out of 20 pregnancies 16 survived infancy. Another said one aunt had 18 pregnancies with 16 survivals. In another context I met a woman reported to be in her 70s who had had 18 pregnancies with 18 live births. This does not mean that all women had high numbers of pregnancies nor that all women were fertile. There are also reports of total family sizes of five and six with indications that this number represented all or most of a woman's pregnancies. In the past women who were infertile (like others in the community) generally adopted children.

The total fertility rate appears to have progressively decreased over the last few decades. As noted earlier, the total fertility rate has decreased from 8.2 in 1973 to 4.3 in 1994 (National Government Federated States of Micronesia, 1996), which is the same as the figure calculated by Flear in 1998. A few women were asked what they thought was the ideal family size today. Most suggested four to five, but some put this in economic terms and said it depends on how many one can afford. Such comments are interesting because in the past large families were often considered more advantageous economically (see for example the comment by A. Fischer [1963, p. 527] for Chuuk); care given to children, along with other goods and services, was expected to be returned to the parents as the children matured.

NOTE

1. There is information that kava was used in other Pacific Island cultures to ease labor. Considering the properties of kava it could be useful.

Chapter 6

Postpartum Motherhood

This section is about only some aspects of motherhood; it focuses primarily on the postpartum period and things that can be associated with it, such as making decisions about birth control and adoption. In this study we did not explore other aspects of motherhood (although some aspects came up regularly), as time did not allow us to address the important topic of motherhood beyond the postpartum in appropriate depth. It is, however, a topic worthy of more detailed exploration. Such a study might explore such things as the meaning of motherhood for women and their families, and ideas about what makes a woman a good mother. The latter may be particularly important, as women regularly suggested that one of the primary reasons for problems with young people today, including teenage pregnancies and drug use, is that mothers (and fathers) are not fulfilling their parental responsibilities.

BELIEFS AND PRACTICES

As with pregnancy and birthing, there were some beliefs and practices associated with the early postpartum period. Again, these beliefs and practices, like the others, were designed to promote the health of the mother and the baby and to protect them from harm. For the most part they focused on supporting the mother's ability to breast-feed her baby and to protect both of them from evil spirits.

Treated Like a Queen

She said that after birth is the best time for a woman. That is because she is treated like a queen. All she has to do is to take care of the baby. This is only to breast-feed her baby. Even to pick up the baby to her breasts, one of the mothers or aunts would do that. All she does other than feeding the baby is to eat, sleep, and rest and look beautiful. We were laughing out loud because of her facial expression. This lady enjoyed staying at home after giving birth to her children.

The new mother was to eat and drink well so she would have enough milk; she should even eat in the middle of the night. She was brought special foods believed to help her develop enough milk. According to many women, during this period, as during pregnancy, the woman was "treated like a queen," she was indulged, and everything was done to keep her happy. She was never left alone during this period, and she was not allowed to be sad.

In the past women were excused from their usual activities for a period of time after childbirth. During this period the new mother was to concentrate on herself and feeding her baby. Often others took on other aspects of infant care and took care of any other children. One woman explained it this way: "she [the mother] wouldn't even lift the child. If she is my mother she will have to give me the child to put on my lap so I can start my breast-feeding."

Women reported varying lengths for this time period, generally from one month or 40 days to several months. One woman said: "Those are the practices of long ago. Now we say never mind. After 14 days I have to go back to my desk."

As this woman's comment makes clear, contemporary women often do not get the opportunity to be treated like a queen, and neither did some women in the past. Two of the women told us they had to resume their everyday activities right after their children were born because they had no one to help them. As noted earlier, in one case the woman's mother had died and in the other the mother was quite old and unable to assist her daughter. One said her sisters-in-law provided periodic assistance, but the other woman said she had no one to help her. So, although ideally the new mother got the opportunity to rest and be pampered for a period after giving birth, this did not apply to all women, even in the past.

There are indications that today even fewer women get this period of pampering. This is not because they do not have mothers, sisters, and mothers-in-law, although this may be the case when women live away from kin in another municipality or another state; more often it seems that this happens when young women are trying to live a modern, independent lifestyle. One woman told us that one of her daughters went from the hospital directly to her own home. She did not want her mother to stay with her, she just wanted her husband and the baby—she wanted to be independent, to do things herself.

There is another reason, however, related to contemporary women's lives. A couple of grandmothers reported that because they work they are not able to spend as much time as they would like with their daughters when they give birth. When the daughters live in another state or overseas, the situation can get even more complicated, because it can be difficult to arrange time away from work at the right time, and even then, they might be able to be away only for a couple of weeks.

If You Can't Be a Queen

One of the older women who did not have an opportunity to be treated like a queen told us about how she managed some things in the first few days after her babies were born. She said that in those days it was OK if she did not get time to rest because she was very strong and healthy; she had taken her local medicines.

> She said that when she delivered her babies, the very day she would get up and start walking around the house. That was how strong she used to feel. Nowadays she feels weak because of her pains in the joints. She said she believes she is experiencing these kinds of problems now because she used to work too much. She was not used to sitting around and do-ing nothing else but watch her baby. She could not do that because she needed to attend to her house chores as a mother should normally do if she does not have a helper at the house. Nowadays she cannot do much because of the pains that she is afraid of. She just stays at the house and depends on her children to take care of things and of her.
>
> What she normally did after delivery, she would get around her house doing her own washing of her dirty clothes, sit around with her baby on her lap, and drink her medicine. Then she would bathe her baby and boil water for herself to bathe with. As soon as the umbilical cord for her baby was healed, she took care of the house chores. That is also when she would start massaging the baby to be strong. Normally the mother waits for the umbilical cord to be healed, but sometimes it takes up to the third month; then the baby starts to get massages.
>
> Mothers start picking up the baby from its bed (which is made of piles of baby wraps or towels right by the mother on her mat or on her bed) and starts to massage before sunrise to make the baby strong. She said these are from her own experiences, and from what she heard from other people. She is not sure if the rest of the Pohnpeian women experienced these kinds of things. But surely, she did these things.

It appears that at least some other children in Pohnpei (e.g., Pohnpeian and Chuukese) were given this kind of massage, if not by mothers then by grandmothers or aunties. In this study we concentrated on the women and not their newborns. As a result, any information we obtained on beliefs and practices associated with the baby was purely fortuitous. This is, however, an area worthy of more attention.

Avoiding Danger

During this period women were not supposed to do certain things. In most cases the purpose was so the new mother and child would not be exposed to potentially harmful spirits or *eni*. In addition to never being alone, the mother should not walk in the rain or let her infant's head get wet, she should not bathe in the streams (or anywhere outside) at night, and she should never walk in the dark—most certainly she should never walk in the dark alone. In fact, women were not encouraged to go outside of the house for the first few weeks except to attend to personal care needs. In all of these situations the woman and her baby were particularly vulnerable to spirit sicknesses. To avoid bad spirits and to keep the mother healthy and keep her from getting lazy, women were often awakened early to bathe, just after sunrise, during pregnancy and in the postpartum period.

One of the most important ways of avoiding danger, including illness, was to keep the mother happy.

> When asked if there were more things to do or not to do, she said that one of the major things to do to the mother is to make sure she is happy. If the mother is happy, the baby will be happy, too, and will not be sick. If the mother is unhappy or sad, the baby will be hungry, as the breasts will be dried up as a result of the mother's sadness. The mothers will always make sure the husband is faithful; he is not fooling around with any other women while he is kept away from his wife. Remember that during this time of childbirth (*neitik*) the husband is not supposed to be with the wife. However, he is not supposed to be wandering around either. He is supposed to be faithful and takes care of the older children. (A little laughter when we talked about the husband being kept away from the wife and yet not allowed to wander around).

Sexual Abstinence

Perhaps the most important restriction and the one women talked about the most was the restriction on sexual activity. One of the primary explanations is that it is necessary to assure the health of the child.

If either parent engaged in sexual activity before the end of the prescribed period or did so without giving the child a protective potion, the child would get diarrhea or develop "colic" and be irritable and cry a lot. But more than the health of the child was involved. According to one of the oldest women, the woman who did not have the strength of will to keep her husband away was endangering her own health.

> She said (and pointed to the porch) that the husband had to sleep on the porch, not with the mom and the baby in her room. She said (with a gesture showing that she definitely had her husband sleep separate from her) that only *kommwad* or "brave" women would dare to sleep with their husbands during those days. We were laughing because she kept emphasizing that really only *kommwad* women would dare to allow their husbands to sleep with them and do whatever they want to their bodies. It is very frightening just to think of what would happen next. The husband would be doing whatever he wants to satisfy himself and then the wife would be the one to suffer the consequences. It is the wife who is supposed to refuse and stop the husband from taking the pleasure in her body. Those women who cannot control themselves and do not have the strong will to stop their husbands are the ones who suffer the consequences and then die later or sooner. It is dangerous to ignore this.

Although this is not what the woman above was talking about, many saw this period of abstinence as a form of birth control that could help with the spacing of a woman's pregnancies and thereby protect her health.

The period of abstinence varied from one month to several years, with four months and one year being commonly reported. One woman said they could not have sex until the child could walk. She said children start to walk at about one year. In some places this period of abstinence could be even longer. For example, some women reported that on Kosrae abstinence lasted until the child could jump over a ditch of a specified distance. This could mean a period of abstinence that might last up to four years. The woman who reported this also jokingly suggested that one might adapt the width of the ditch depending on when one was ready to resume having sex.

To help ensure that the mother did not have sex, her mother and, according to some, other women such as the mother-in-law, midwife, and possibly aunties, slept near the new mother. One woman said all these women slept outside the door of the new mother's room, acting as a barrier. If the husband wanted to get to his wife, he had to climb over several adult women and had to deal with them if they woke.

Some told us that the husband was not even allowed to see his wife for as long as a month after childbirth.

Younger women, according to both their reports and that of older women, often do not practice a period of abstinence. One young woman said she was not even aware that she should not sleep with her husband until one of the older women in the family scolded her for doing so. She clearly could not understand why she should not sleep with her husband and continued to do so.

Food Dos and Don'ts

One of the ways new mothers were kept happy was for the family to provide enough food to eat.

> Maureen asked if women ever got sad for other reasons than their husbands fooling around. According to this woman, there are times the mother is sad when there is no meat. "Everyday meat" was fish. Sometimes there were local chickens, and local porks, etc. If the food is served without any meat, the mother feels upset or sad. It was believed that meat makes the food go well when eaten; therefore, if there was no meat, the mother felt upset and sad.
>
> Sometimes also when there is not enough food to eat, the mothers feel sad because their babies will not eat enough from her breasts. When the mother does not eat well, the baby will not be fed well and will eventually become a skinny and small baby. This will also make a baby very fussy, not sleep well, and always cries, as he/she is not satisfied when fed with the breasts.
>
> She said that when a baby is well fed and full, he/she always sleeps and is satiated. Otherwise, if the baby doesn't eat well and is not satisfied with his/her milk, it will cry and cry all day long and night long, which will eventually depress the mother and make her feel so tired and sick also.

The following summary from one interview covers most of the information we collected on the kinds of food women should and should not eat in the early postpartum period and, apparently, while she engaged in breast-feeding. Women were encouraged to drink a lot and eat foods thought to stimulate the production of breast milk. This included, for example, foods that resembled breast milk, such as coconut milk.

> For instance, octopus is one of the meats that is advised not to eat. That is because they believe that if the mother eats it, the baby might have skin rash from that. They believe that the juice causes some kind of irritation on the skin. Sashimi (raw fish) is also not good to be eaten. All these things are irritating to the skin of the baby as well as inside the fresh wound in the uterus of the mother. To feed the mother good food in order to have full breasts for the baby, the mother even has to eat at nighttime so that she can feel strong.

The best foods are those with coconut milk. Soup is good, too. Frying and barbecue are not advisable. They also advised to drink a lot of water, coconut drinks, but again, anything with coconut milk is the best.

This woman expressed the importance of eating with coconut milk as well as the drinking of lots of water and coconut drinks by putting strong emphases on those words.

She also said that there were local medicines they prepared for the mother and the baby to drink, which were like vitamins.

Several women mentioned that a particular kind of clam was especially important for new mothers because it helped with the development of breast milk. Obtaining these clams was a job for the new father. This was one food that many expected for the birth feast.

Birth Feast—*uhmwen ipwidi*

Soon after the baby is born the family has a feast.

This one they called it *uhmwen ipwiti*. [According to Barnabas and Hezel (1993) it was called *pilendihdi* and Kihleng (1992) *uhmw en pilen dihdi*. For a firstborn child on Pingelap it is called *kamadipu in meseni* (Ashby, 1983b, p. 31).] Then during the fourth day after birth, there is another one, which is called *kemen sapw*. Nowadays, she cannot do those things because there are too many children for her to feed. Especially those feasts have to have pigs and such. She said, "Where will I get all the pigs from?" for all the feasts. Before it was OK because people liked to tend to their own farms and raised pigs, chickens, etc. Nowadays, kids are in school, no one around to help to do the chores. The new lifestyle really changes everything.

What is the purpose of the feast after the fourth day?

She said that it is specially for both the mother and baby because now the mother is supposed to feel stronger and the umbilical cord is supposed to be healing well.

During this particular feast, the relatives bring a lot of food, especially the sea clams, which are best for breast-feeding. Nowadays, no more. Mothers deliver their babies, and all they do is bring chickens from the freezer and prepare for her.

Ashby's description is consistent with that provided by these women:

All celebrations, food donated and gifts presented after the birth of the child are called *pilen dihdi*, or watery breast.[1] In the past, the term referred only to gifts that could be consumed.

When the mother regains her strength, a ceremony is held, and the husband is responsible for organizing it. Members of the family must fish for four days, and search particularly for two types of shellfish and clams:

kemei and *lipwei*. These are thought to develop rich milk in the mother's breasts. Those who remain behind prepare local foods for the large feast that is held.

At a time following the fourth day after the birth, the family will usually take the child to be baptized at either a Catholic or Protestant church. After baptism, another feast takes place. (Ashby, 1983a, pp. 188–189)

Although Baranbas and Hezel (1993) suggest that this practice is less common because changes in health care increase the potential for mother and infant survival and first birthday feasts may have replaced this celebration, Kihleng's work suggests that the *uhmw en pilen dihdi* continues. Kihleng (1996) reports that four days after the birth a feast is given to honor the new mother.

The feast, *uhmw en pilen dihdi*, literally "stone oven of breast milk," . . . is sponsored by the young woman's parents. In the present day context, the feast may not necessarily entail a stone oven, but may instead consist of iron pots of cooked food, or perhaps, both. This depends on the wishes and, more importantly, the financial considerations of the woman's parents. . . .

The feast begins with the ritual bathing of the new mother by her own mother and other matrilineal kinswomen. A large basin filled with hot water that is mixed with certain medicinal leaves is prepared. The young woman sits in the basin and is rinsed with the water, using a *lihmw* (sponge) that is gathered especially for this ritual. [See also Local Medicine below.] After the bath the young woman is rubbed with coconut oil that is mixed with tumeric. The ritualistic bath and anointment are said to cleanse the young woman after the birth, and to make her skin smooth and beautiful. Their practice is also believed to prevent her skin from becoming dark. . . . After the ritual is completed, the new mother is dressed, most often in a beautifully designed and colorful appliqued skirt (*urohs*) and is then ready to greet the female participants who are waiting to present her with various gifts.

Some women described a feast or ceremony that is similar to that described by Ashby as *uhm-mwin neitik*, which occurs "when a mother regains her strength" (Ashby, 1983b, p. 28). They may both be talking about what the women seemed to refer to as the birth feast, but in the past at least, there may have been two events: one immediately after the birth and one four days later (or, according to Ashby [1983b], at ten days on Mokil and eight days on Pingelap). Or perhaps, what they mean is that there is a feast that lasts four days, something at least one of the women indicated. This would be consistent with feast descriptions described by Kihleng (1996).

The person responsible for this occasion will be the husband. Foods necessary at this time include yams, breadfruit, and fresh meat or fish. Many activities take place at *uhn-mwin netik*. Members of the family will go fishing for four days and will search particularly for two types of shellfish known as "kemei" and "lipwei" in Ponapean. These are known to be helpful for developing rich milk in the mother's breast. After four days of fishing, a feast will be held. Those who remained behind will contribute and prepare food while the fishermen will present their catch. (Ashby, 1983b, p. 28)

Ashby goes on to note that

The families of the couple are expected to visit the new mother and bring gifts, and it is shameful to arrive without a contribution of some sort. This is done only for the first-born child, however. All gifts are accepted and they might include imported articles or locally made items. Some visitors might bring long woven baskets containing a cooked pig, or dog, yams, or breadfruit. The husband will see to it that the local drink, "sakau," is provided. (Ashby, 1983b, p. 28)

Today, among those gifts are brightly colored towels that are used as baby wraps. The presence of these towels allowed me to quickly tell whether the clinics I observed on particular days included postnatal visits. Kihleng (1996, pp. 288–289) notes that the list of gifts can include "towels, buckets, laundry detergent and soap, diapers, baby clothes and blankets, and bath soap as well as various foodstuffs and money."

Yasuo (1940) says that a *kamateppu* or banquet is held only for the first birth. Statements by some of the women we interviewed suggest that this was especially important for a first child but that a small feast might occur with subsequent children.

Breast and Abdominal Binding

Some of the women talked about abdominal binding as something women did in the past. Generally women in their 40s either did not mention abdominal binding or told us they did not do it, even if their mothers told them they should. One woman said that her mother told her to bind her abdomen, but that she "was lazy at that time," and did not do it. These women think the binding helped older women keep their shape, their flat stomachs, even when they had multiple pregnancies.

A couple of women also mentioned breast binding, but the reason for this was given as assisting with the production of milk. One woman said that if the breasts hang loose the woman will lose her milk.

Breast-Feeding

Many of the practices associated with the postpartum period had to do with encouraging the production of breast milk. As already noted, women were encouraged to eat and drink a lot. They were even expected to eat during the night. They were also encouraged to eat particular kinds of foods, especially a certain kind of clam. The woman's husband was expected to go out and collect some of these clams for his wife to help her produce high-quality breast milk that would help make the baby strong.

One woman, using information she had acquired more recently about diet, particularly eating large quantities of food and its effects on health, suggested that this practice of encouraging new mothers to eat lots of food was probably not a good thing by today's standards. In fact, she suggested that it may have contributed to some of the health problems women have today that are associated with diet and obesity.

> But when we come to know that even if you eat trays of food it doesn't affect here [the breast]. It affects the body to grow bigger. But they practice long ago. They give you. You even, 12 o'clock even you eat. They believe that. Eat food so the baby will become strong. We hadn't learned about these things. We eat, drink. It only make us sick. (laugh)

Introduction of Other Foods

Most women reported exclusive breast-feeding for the first five to six months. "It all depends on how long the mother can breast-feed" and the quality of her milk. One woman reported that she introduced soft food at two to three months, and another said she added other foods at eight to nine months. The latter woman told us that one of her daughters had her baby at the hospital and that they fed the baby with baby food the day after she was discharged. However, for most children other foods were slowly introduced. One woman said that for her first child, she added solid foods at two months because "the nurse advised her to. . . . The others started to eat at six months."

Apparently the introduction of solid food at five to seven months was fairly common. One of these foods, known as the *karat* banana, is particularly high in vitamin A (L. Englberger, personal communication, July 1999).[2] This banana, which is deep orange in color, has a very soft consistency. It is spoken of within these interviews and some of the literature as a "weaning" food and as a food for babies and pigs. Other foods such as bananas, ripe papaya, taro, and breadfruit could also be used. These foods were either mashed into a paste-like consistency or premasticated to the appropriate texture. One woman noted that these foods might be mashed with coconut milk to make them the right consistency. Originally from one of the outer islands, this woman suggested that when these foods were introduced, the child might also begin to drink "soft coconuts." She noted that young babies were not given meat.

> They would not feed the baby with any kind of meat. She said meat was discouraged for babies at that early stage because during that time, meat was scarce. Usually they would mostly eat fish, sometimes local pork or chicken. Unfortunately, there were times they would run out of meat. Therefore, it was advised that newborn was better off without meat. Otherwise, the baby would be unhappy when meat was not served, and parents would not want their babies to be disappointed because of that. They would rather feed the baby with those local produce such as taros and breadfruits than with meat. (See also Demory, 1976, p. 67)

I had the distinct impression that the women who breast-fed, particularly the older women, did not supplement the breast-feeding in any way during the early months. However, L. Englberger (personal communication, December 2000 and January 2001) and some others suggest that this is not the case and never was, that infants in Pohnpei are rarely exclusively breast-fed. According to L. Englberger's informants, there has been the belief in the past that colostrum was considered dirty and was thrown away. This belief is less common today because the health service teaches that colostrum is good and should be given. Women regularly give their infants liquids such as water from the time of birth and may introduce other foods quite early. She reports that in Kosrae at least "they believe that something must be given to babies for a drink, that all people have to drink something and so they believe that the babies need to drink something too, and that there is nothing cleaner than coconut juice—so that is commonly given" (L. Englberger, personal communication, December 2000).

Ashby says, "The mother would not begin feeding the newly born infant immediately. The baby was first given a liquid called *kourapw*, a lubricant made from coconut oil. It was believed that when a child was first born, its intestines were not completely open and *kourapw* would help open the intestines for the mother's milk" (Ashby, 1983b, p. 27).

According to Yasuo (1940, p. 13 of English language reprint), coconut meat, coconut syrup, bananas, and sugarcane sap were all used as "substitutes of mother's milk."

I asked some of my key informants if they agreed with this. The following is an excerpt from my field notes on an informal key informant interview.

Apparently women may give water even during the early days, but I am assured no food and definitely not coconut. I got the idea that coconut is totally improper for very young infants. The water is given or can be given in various ways. It can be dripped from the fingers, or a cup, or the mother might give it to the baby from her mouth. I can't remember but there was also something that could be used as a sort of funnel to give water and a bottle was mentioned, but that was not the first thing mentioned. I have the distinct impression that other foods are generally not introduced until at least 3 months, but it all depends on the quality and quantity of the mother's milk. Oh, there was also a brief mention of wet nursing in the past, but that it is not used often now. [Name] had mentioned that the other day as well. It also seems to depend on the baby and if the baby seems satisfied. So it looked like three to six months is common for the introduction of other foods, including premasticated foods.

One of the informants at the hospital reported that today, except in unusual circumstances, all babies are put to the breast as soon as they are born. Today, as a general rule, infants are given nothing but the breast while the mother and infant are in the hospital. The staff discourage mothers from giving anything but the breast until they believe it is time to introduce solid food. This appears to be a fairly recent policy position, one introduced in the last few years. Prior to that time newborns were often given plain water or "sugar water" from a bottle in the first 24 hours or until breast-feeding or bottle-feeding was well established. In the past, women who wanted to bottle-feed could do so if they brought their own bottles to the hospital. Today, if a woman brings bottles to the hospital the staff will "talk to her" about the advantages of breast-feeding, and most women are, according to one informant, soon "convinced" that breast-feeding is the better option.

For many years in U.S. hospitals, babies were given only "sugar water" for the first feeding and sometimes for the first 24 hours or so. Reasons for this included waiting for the mother's milk to come in (this was before the benefits of colostrum were scientifically identified), giving the mother a period to recover (especially if an anesthetic or difficult delivery was involved), and making sure the baby was able to suckle without difficulty. Giving water or coconut water in the immediate postnatal period is also reported in some cases in Samoa, for much the same reasons as just noted.

From this data it is not clear whether or not the early introduction of supplements is a long-standing practice. As with other things, there was probably some variability. And perhaps, some women do not consider giving water or coconut water as supplementation; it might not be considered as food and thus, not a supplement to the breast. These women clearly identified breast milk as the baby's food.

Length of Breast-Feeding

Reports vary on the length of time women would breast-feed, anything from six months to several years. Demory (1976, p. 67) says babies were "usually weaned from the breast between nine and fifteen months." If a woman became pregnant, she stopped breast-feeding the nursing child. As many women reported a pregnancy a year, it is very likely that many children were weaned when they were less than a year old. Demory (1976) reports that women gave several reasons for stopping breast-feeding: "there was no more milk, the milk turned bad, the baby didn't want milk, or the mother was tired of feeding the baby. Today it is becoming increasingly common to wean the baby from breast to bottle at six to seven months for the same reason." Demory also notes that at the time of her study, the 1970s, women who were still in school or had a job often did not breast-feed at all. At the time of her study, she says, the incidence of severe malnutrition was the highest around the time a child was weaned from the breast.

Lactation Was Not a Contraceptive

Women also reported that breast-feeding did not provide protection against becoming pregnant. They cited their frequent pregnancies as evidence that breast-feeding does not act as a natural contraceptive. The older woman who told us she did not introduce other foods until her children were eight to nine months old commented that "even though I kept on breast-feeding I still got pregnant every year." The only time there was more than one year between her children was between a child by her first husband, who died, and the next child, whose father was the man she married a couple of years later.

This information is consistent with that found among Samoans (Fitzgerald, 1992) and contrary to that presented in various educational publications, including some specific for Pacific populations. These interview data offer further evidence that lactation, even intensive, on-demand breast-feeding (whether or not other liquids are given in the first 24 hours), is not a natural contraceptive among healthy and/or robust populations. As I have pointed out elsewhere (Fitzgerald, 1992), and these women noted, women in these populations who want to avoid unwanted pregnancies must begin family planning early after delivery, even if they are intensively lactating. They should not wait until they have their first postpartum period, nor should they wait until they introduce solid food or decide to wean their baby from the breast.

Bottle-Feeding

Some women reported having used bottle-feeding.[3] At one time, in both the United States and the Pacific it was viewed as the preferred form of infant feeding. It was seen as modern and of higher quality than the breast, which was for those who could not afford bottles and formula. There was no doubt that the women are well aware that things have changed. They now see breast-feeding as the preferred method. Younger women are aware of the "baby-friendly hospital" concept being promoted in FSM. This program actively discourages bottle-feeding and does not allow bottle-feeding in the hospital after childbirth except in extreme circumstances.

One of the younger women reported that she had problems getting her infant to breast-feed. When she went home she continued to try to get him to take the breast, but after a week she went back to the hospital and told them, "Every night he just cried and cried and cried. He doesn't sleep. He sleeps for maybe about 15 minutes and then cries. And when I feed him then he just. . . . And they say just try. [Finally,] even though they don't like to bottle-feed, they told me to try and bottle-feed."

During this discussion, this young woman expressed concern about her baby, and her questions about her difficulty in getting her infant to nurse suggested that she might have been trying to figure out whether it was her or her baby who had failed the breast-feeding expectation. This and other discussions during the period of data collection suggest that some caution must be exercised in the breast-feeding and "baby-friendly hospital" promotions. Women who are unable to achieve the current "ideal" in infant feeding may encounter feelings of inadequacy every bit as powerful and devastating as the feelings once associated with not being able to bottle-feed. Promoting breast-feeding and infant and child health should not be accomplished at the expense of new mothers' senses of adequacy.

One of the women in her 60s told us that only her youngest child was bottle-fed. They had to bottle-feed her because the woman was sent to Kolonia for an operation. This woman said her relationship with this child is different because she was bottle-fed.

> Because of this bottle-feeding process, she believes that is the reason why her daughter is very *ketihwo*, or naughty, mischievous or hard to deal with. She said she is staying on [another island], and she does not seem to miss anyone at home. She has been gone for a while. The rest of her children were breast-fed and seemed to be very close to her. She believes that breast-feeding is something that binds the mother to the children.

There is a strong bond there. Her young daughter while she was on Pohnpei, even when her mother and other siblings are here on the island including herself, she would prefer to be staying with her aunts or other relatives. She stayed with her aunt until the day she was leaving to [the other island].

We were laughing because she was saying that her husband said this young daughter of theirs surely has a life and heart of a cow. We laughed and asked her why a cow, and she said it is the same as an animal and cow is what she was fed from.

Local Medicine

Women, at least in the past and perhaps even today, used local medicine after childbirth to "clean out" the uterus—and many continued to use their traditional tonics. A couple of women told us that they "used to boil water, soak a piece of cloth in it, and sort of pad around the vagina with the warm cloth or small towel." According to one woman, they "used to place the soaked piece of cloth right into the hole to help clean out inside the cervix. That was to clean and help heal the wound faster. . . . Sometimes the women cleaned without hot water. They got sick from infection and that is how some of the women ended up having cervical cancer."

POTENTIAL POSTPARTUM ILLNESSES

As already noted, the term *ohn neitik* (childbirth hangover) can be used to refer to the pains associated with giving birth (R.L. Ward, 1977, pp. 68–69). However, Ward notes that the former has more to do with difficulties that occur after delivery and in the postnatal period. These include symptoms such as loss of appetite and weight, malaise, and fatigue. Because these feelings are similar to those associated with the after-effects of a drinking bout, people often use the word *ohn* (*ohn sakau* or kava hangover) to describe this state. R.L. Ward (1977) also mentions a minor ailment, *mehn do* (soreness of the breasts), which can occur during either pregnancy or nursing.

Women were asked if any illnesses were associated with the period after birth. Clearly some of the practices during pregnancy, such as the Seventh-Month Feast, recognized that the period surrounding childbirth is a dangerous time for women and their newborns. Most women claimed no specific illnesses were associated with the postpartum period, but obviously many of the practices during the period were designed to assure the woman's health—as well as that of her child.

Spirit Sickness—*soumwauen eni*

Spirit sickness or *soumwauen eni* was discussed earlier in the context of potential illnesses during pregnancy (see also Chapter 4). Such illnesses could also occur during the postpartum period. Again, the family would generally use the services of a local healer if they suspected a spirit sickness.

Other Illnesses or Health Concerns

One of the women referred to earlier regarding spirit sickness during pregnancy reported the following (from a summary transcript):

> Of course, some young mothers experienced some types of sicknesses which the families always tried to find cures for them. As she mentioned earlier, whatever sickness it might be, the family always tried its best to find cures for it. If they do not know the medicine themselves, they would go to the nearby neighbors or other families who might know how to cure it.

In an attempt to obtain more information on such "sicknesses" the woman was asked about a specific situation that may occur after childbirth. She was asked "if bleeding was common with young mothers after birth."

> *Inta kereker* is what they call it when a mother is losing too much blood. Yes, that was one of the major causes of death. Some women used to die when they lost too much blood. She said that sometimes the mother might lose too much blood even before delivery and that became fatal to both she and the baby in her womb if she lost it. And, if she loses blood during delivery, it also threatens the family so they would try to find medicines to stop it. It is a life-threatening situation.

Again, as noted earlier, "In order to drive away the evil spirits, there is a special way to apply the medicinal herb. Someone among the women (local healers) would chew the herb and spread it all over the body of the sick woman by blowing out the chewed herbs all over her. This term is called *purak*."

The response we got to this specific question suggests that in future studies, the open-ended questions regarding illnesses might usefully be followed by questions on specific conditions commonly associated with pregnancy and childbirth in other contexts, such as Western biomedicine. We did not commonly ask such questions in this preliminary and exploratory study. In this case, as this was a second interview with this woman and the discussion had moved into the area of health, illness, and healing, the question seemed appropriate. The woman had already seen that I was interested in such topics and that I received such information in a nonjudgmental way. This type of rapport may be required to obtain more information of this type.

The women did not really discuss infections of any kind during the postpartum period, although in more general terms some talked about the importance of good hygiene and the importance of using "boiled water" to cleanse the woman's private areas so she would not get an infection. I can find no references in the transcripts to problems such as infections or breast tenderness during the postpartum period. Such problems most certainly must have occurred at least occasionally; they are mentioned by R.L. Ward (1977). I suspect they were not mentioned because we did not ask the questions in the right way, or perhaps this was simply an area of knowledge the women decided to hold back for now.

Illnesses in the Newborn

Although we did not specifically discuss issues associated with beliefs and practices in terms of the newborn child, it was clear that the behaviors of the mother, father, and family were important for ensuring the health and well-being of the unborn child. If a child was born with some type of impairment or birth defect, people explored both the behaviors of all the core people and relationships within the family and between the family and its neighbors.

Of course, many other beliefs and practices are specially associated with newborns, which is another topic worthy of study. The kinds of information we obtained in terms of newborns were offered in the context of talk on other topics. For example, one woman told us that a woman should never carry her baby so that it faced backward over her shoulder.

> The reason why you cannot do these things with the baby is that the baby might see ghosts behind you that might make him/her sick. They always believe in ghosts that everywhere they go, they have to make sure the babies are protected from them. A mother is supposed to carry her baby and make sure the baby is facing forward so the ghosts from behind would not scare him/her.

Postnatal Mental Health

There is no evidence that postnatal depression, postnatal psychosis, or even the "baby blues" have ever been a significant concern in Pohnpei.

There is no evidence of an indigenous illness category with any similarity. One obstetrician reported that at most he may have encountered three cases of postnatal depression during roughly five years of professional experience in Pohnpei. If postnatal depression or psychosis was ever present, it was probably very rare.

I was told only one story that suggested a possible case of postnatal depression; however, the story may have been more myth than the rendition of an actual situation. This story was not presented as a case of postnatal depression but was offered to suggest that maybe something like it may have existed. The case is actually about a spirit possession that occurred because the woman had been left alone. The mother and her baby are left alone in her house for a significant period of time—hours at least. She is holding her baby and having strange thoughts. Suddenly she gets the urge to bite and eat her baby. As she "makes like to eat the baby" she realizes that what she is doing is wrong and she dies. The story seems to serve more as a reminder that new mothers should not be left alone—terrible things can happen, and in this case the family was responsible.

After hearing this story I asked people if there were any cases of new mothers hurting their infants. Despite much evidence of concern about child abuse (e.g., posters in public places and comments in some recent publications) and that child abuse and neglect has increased in Micronesia (e.g., Marcus, 1991; Rubinstein, 1994) everyone denied that there had ever been a case of a new mother abusing a young infant. One person suggested that neglect was more likely to occur than direct physical abuse, a point consistent with the work of Marcus (1991). As Marcus notes, terms such as *abuse* and *neglect* may have different meanings in Micronesia if such things are judged by community standards rather than some U.S.-based or international definitions. Marcus defines neglect as "the failure of parents or guardians to provide what they could be expected to provide in terms of food, clothing, medical care, and general support" (Marcus, 1991, p. 3).

Traditional postnatal practices would seem to have provided the kind of supportive environment that would protect women from postnatal depression or the opportunity to harm their infants even if they were so inclined. After a birth, a woman was a focus of attention for a significant period of time. Others catered to her needs and desires and did everything they could to keep the new mother "happy." The mother had assistance with baby and child care during the early postnatal period, and this assistance potentially could last for several months. The woman in the story above had been left alone.

The frequent comments about keeping the mother happy might be stretched to suggest that postnatal depression was an issue and that these measures were designed as a kind of preventive measure. This support was very likely a preventive measure but probably of a more unintentional nature. It is more likely that such measures were designed to support breast-feeding. The ability to breast-feed, particularly in terms of having sufficient milk, appears to have been of some concern. Women talked a lot about how new mothers were encouraged to eat and drink a lot and to eat food identified as assisting the production of breast milk. Keeping mothers relaxed and providing them with the support of women with significant breast-feeding experience (mothers, mothers-in-law, midwives) would certainly have helped. In fact, it seems that today much of this support is being replaced by nonfamily members, such as doctors and nurses, as is the situation among many other populations, including those in developed societies (e.g., Davis-Floyd & Sargent, 1997; Fitzgerald, 1995; Fitzgerald et al., 1998; Jordan, 1993; Ram & Jolly, 1998).

"Feeling Bad Sickness"—*soumwau en insensued*

As noted earlier, concerns about a husband's fidelity were viewed as something that could cause a young mother distress. R.L. Ward calls this condition "feeling bad sickness" or *soumwau en insensued* (see also Chapter 4). If there is a Pohnpeian cognate condition with postnatal depression, this might be a possibility, although it is not necessarily primarily associated with pregnancy or the postnatal period.

The following, an excerpt from my field notes, is from an interview with a Chuukese informant, but it is consistent with the reports from women from other cultural groups in Pohnpei.

> If the husband went off and had sex, then the child would develop diarrhea. This was a sign of the husband's infidelity. It would have to be the husband because the mother was sleeping with her daughter. If this happened the mother and grandmother would keep at the daughter, telling her the child was sick because the husband was going with other women. This would cause great emotional distress for the young mother. She would be upset because her husband was not being faithful. There is much worry about husbands straying during this long period of abstinence. A man who is faithful must really love his wife. If the husband and wife have sex before it is time, the child may end up with colic, a baby that cries all the time. Before the parents resume sex after the period of prescribed abstinence (or thereabouts) they give the child an herbal preparation to protect it from getting sick.

If, however, the mother knew her husband was actually having an affair, she confronted the woman and got a piece of her hair any way she could, including tearing it from her head in a physical confrontation. This hair was then burned and used as part of the ritual cure for the child.

Cultural Change and a Context for Illness

Some of the things women associated with cultural change suggest that perhaps these changes are resulting in a context in which postnatal distress or illness might become more common. As already noted, the usual support system following childbirth is not always available. Grandmothers have to return to their jobs, women may live far away from female kin or live in nuclear family households, and some may choose not to follow traditional practices.

> She said there are times that her daughters feel sad during childbirth. It is when they are tired of taking care of their babies. Because nowadays the daughters are attending to their own babies. The mother stays for only a short time, like up to a month, to help her daughter and then leaves to go to her own home. Nowadays, most daughters either share the home of her husband's family or have a home of her own with her husband and children, instead of with her own mother and father.

As noted earlier, one young woman reported during an informal interview that young women who are not allowed to return to school after childbirth may become depressed. In part this is because it can close off future employment opportunities and, perhaps of more immediate significance, it takes the woman out of her circle of friends and the life of a young woman without major responsibilities. One result is that these women can begin to feel isolated and shunned by former friends and burdened by adult responsibilities. This does not mean that all school-age new mothers feel this way, but apparently, some do. Other young mothers welcome marriage and pregnancy and the assumption of a more adultlike life.

The currently available data do not indicate that postnatal depression is an obvious or significant illness in Pohnpei today. On the other hand, in this preliminary short-term background study we collected little information from mothers in the early postnatal period, the women who would be at the greatest risk for such mental health concerns.

The data do suggest, however, that there is an increased risk for such problems. Traditional support systems are no longer as strong as in the past. Young women live more isolated lives than the generation before them (see also Falgout, 1993). The period of "adolescence" has been extended to include at least the high school years, if not college. This means that getting married in one's teen years and/or having babies then is no longer as acceptable as it might have been in earlier generations. Smaller families and prolonged periods of schooling, particularly when this occurs off-island, decrease the amount of experience young women have with child rearing. As I have noted elsewhere (Fitzgerald, 1995), young women in many societies, Western and otherwise, no longer move into motherhood with significant mothering experience. This places many of these young women at risk for mental health concerns.

INFERTILITY, BIRTH SPACING, AND MULTIPLE BIRTHS

We asked a couple of the women why some women have only a few children or no children at all. The issue of infertility also came up in another interview involving two other women. In this case none of us was referring to the use of birth control. We were talking about women who never had children and those who had long periods of time between pregnancies that could not be explained by abstinence or the use of birth control (none of the women considered lactation as a contraceptive of any note) (see also Fitzgerald, 1992). In one interview this discussion led into a discussion of multiple births. Infertility and natural birth spacing were also discussed in some casual interviews with others in the community.

> According to this lady, she said that some believe they are sick. That is why they either have no child or one or two children. They suspect it could be sickness of the uterus or somewhere within the womb. For example, she said that one of her sisters has a problem with her uterus. That is why she had only one child. Others, they believe it is because some of their ancestors were like that, so they think they inherit that from them.
>
> They also said that it is the same way with those who have twins. Those who have twins in their families, it is possible that the children will also have twins later when they have their children.

A woman involved in another interview thought there was a relationship between irregular menses and infertility (see also Chapter 3). One woman's discussion suggested that perhaps infertility was a form of punishment for bad behavior. One woman had adopted children in the hope that once she had children, she might become pregnant (see also Yasuo, 1940).

Most of the women's explanations were grounded in biological explanations, primarily genetics or illnesses of the uterus. Social, moral, and supernatural explanations were the exception rather than the rule.

Some of the medical people suggested that some infertility is the result of sexually transmitted diseases and pelvic inflammatory disease. One doctor reported that there was a very high incidence of trichomonas among women in Pohnpei. Such explanations are consistent with explanations offered for earlier periods in Micronesian history, particularly the postcontact period, when decreased fertility was often associated with venereal disease.

Others had no explanation for the amount of time between their children. One woman with eight years between her second and third child simply said that when she got pregnant with the youngest child, it was like a first-time pregnancy, because it had been so long since the last pregnancy.

According to some key informants, twins are not unusual in Pohnpei, but triplets are. If a family has a history of twins, then twins are a likely happening. Same-sex twins did not seem to present any problems at all, but in the past at least, one boy and one girl made people a bit uncomfortable. One woman told us:

> There is also a traditional belief that when the set of twins is a boy and a girl, one of them will not live. And also, because long ago, it was not good for a sister and a brother to sit very close together, and therefore, it was also something people shied to even think of that the set of twins apparently came out from the same sack.
>
> For example, when a mother gives birth to this kind of set of twins, people would generally talk about it, and then if someone happens to ask, "and what are they—baby girls or baby boys?" And someone might answer, "a boy and a girl." And then the people might give this "Ooh" expression, which normally, you understand that it is not a sign of excitement, but rather, it gives you a sense of "maybe something is wrong."
>
> Normally, Mother Nature takes its own doing, and creating the set of twins that way is one of its creations. Well, traditionally, that is something people used to feel threatened from. They also believed that those two siblings usually do not get along as well as those twins with same sexes.
>
> If these boy and girl [twins] live, they have bad tempers, too.

Adoption

Hezel (personal communication, July 1999) makes a distinction between adoption and fosterage (see also Carroll, 1970). Hezel equates adoption with "letting the child out to someone in another lineage. Fosterage meant turning the child over to someone in one's own lineage, e.g., the mother's sister or her mother." Hezel (personal communication, September 2000) reports that there does not seem to be a distinct term for adoption in Pohnpeian as there is in Chuukese. Carroll (1970, p. 7) notes that the contributors to his volume on adoption in Oceania generally used *fosterage* to mean "temporarily taking care of others' children as an obligation of kinship" and *adoption* as "permanently assuming the major responsibility of natural parents," but he then goes on to say that a definitive definition of adoption has been elusive. Because the people I talked with during this study generally used the term *adoption* (in English) as a term that would incorporate both fosterage and adoption using the definitions above, I have generally used it as they have, as a generic concept that involves the transfer of some parental rights and expectations for a period of time, whether or not this transfer involves formal or legal acts.

As in other Micronesian communities (Marshall, 1999), all accounts of Pohnpeian culture note that adoption and fosterage were extremely common in the past (e.g., Barnabas & Hezel, 1993; Carroll, 1970; J.L. Fischer, 1970; Kihleng, 1996; M.C. Ward, 1989), but that it was unusual for children to be adopted by total strangers (Carroll, 1970). The people interviewed during this study also noted that adoption, frequently referred to as "sharing children," was very common in the past. My informants and the literature have offered many explanations for why adoption was so common. They include keeping prized land (or other valuables such as titles) within the family; childlessness; not having a child available to care for older adults or to do critical work around a homestead; strengthening ties between individuals, families, or lineages; and just a love of having many children around. In this context, and because Pohnpei is a matrilineal society, children born out of wedlock had a place in society even if they were not adopted; however, in such situations it was common for such children to be adopted, generally by someone within the lineage, frequently an older sibling (see also Barnabas & Hezel, 1993; J.L. Fischer, 1970; M.C. Ward, 1989).

> According to this lady, adoption was something more or less like an exchange for trust. For example, two individuals meet and become friends. In order to show that the relationship was something to be considered permanent, one of the individuals may give up a child to the other so that the child will seal the trust between those two. From that day on, those two become brothers or sisters. This was something that nobody questioned of its validity, and therefore, no legal written documentation was necessary.

These comments are similar to those offered by another woman:

> During those days, people used to like to get to know each other. Unfortunately, in those days transportation was not easy. When they had an

opportunity to meet, people gathered together, for example, people from one municipality going to visit another municipality, and during this kind of occasion, they met and made friends. Then one person would become very close to another person from a different municipality—so close that they even came up with the idea of exchanging children to seal that bond. That was how they practiced adoption.

In some cases there was a sort of formality involved. For example the adoption might be marked by giving the child a plot of land, but more often adoptions were more informal. "She said that during those days, people who were given up for adoption were given the privilege to own pieces of land from their foster parents. That is because as soon as they are adopted, they are given a piece of land from that foster family."

Children knew and had relationships with biological parents as well as adoptive parents. They could generally move between households with ease. If any difficulties arose it might be after an adoptive parent died, when there might be a conflict over who should inherit land. "Although those children given up for adoption may one day come back to their biological families if they desired without any hard feelings, sometimes the children might only visit the families and go back."

Several people suggested that in the contemporary context, the issue of inheriting of land and access to other valued things such as health insurance, compensation packages, and social security benefits have changed the nature of adoption in Pohnpei. These people suggest that adoptions are more often formalized today than in the past because people have to be able to legally demonstrate a relationship to inherit land or gain access to other forms of wealth.

The difference between nowadays and before is that before there was no need to legalize their adoption process. They could just take the child and once the child moves in with that family and became accepted as a member of that family, the adoption process is already done. There was never any problem of adoption during those days. I mean, once a child is given up to another family, the child is considered adopted, which required no written agreement or anything to legalize the adoption. It is already understood and accepted by both parties.

Nowadays, we are required to legalize the adoption because of the new legal system which requires everything to be in written form.

Other factors are said to affect adoption today. One of these factors is that more people work outside of the household than in the past. This means it is more difficult for employed older people, such as parents, grandparents, and older siblings, to assume the care of a baby or young child. Social change and the struggle for money has led to what Marcus (1991) calls the "busy parents" syndrome that not only leads to a reluctance to adopt children but also may lead to child abuse or neglect. Furthermore, according to some informants, many people simply do not want to take on the additional responsibility of another child—doing so has important financial and lifestyle implications in modern Pohnpei.

Although some young women today, in particular young and unmarried women, do give their babies for adoption for the reasons just cited, this is perhaps less common than in the past. In fact, Barnabas and Hezel (1993, p. 10) suggest that "adoption has declined enormously in the present day." Based on our interview data, young women who get pregnant are more likely to be expected to give up school or employment to take care of their own infants than have them cared for or adopted by kin.

People talked about a somewhat new phenomenon in the area of adoption. This is the legal adoption of a child by "strangers" or people outside of the lineage, even people of non-Pohnpeian background. People refer to this as "throwing away" the baby. This type of adoption is formal and follows legal guidelines so that the mother gives up all rights in regard to the child. Such children could be, and sometimes are, legally taken from Pohnpei. Such adoptions did occur in the past, but according to these informants are more common now and almost exclusively associated with unwed (often "wild") women. It was quite obvious that no one who talked about such adoptions approved of them. For many this was just more evidence of the moral decay of Pohnpeian life and society (see Chapter 8). [4]

Although anyone could ask for a child, in the past the mother had some say about whether or not the child would be adopted.

> She herself does not believe in adoption. She said people did have their children adopted. She believes people used to adopt children basically to share the responsibilities. Although her sisters wanted to do that, she told them that the children were her gifts from the Lord so she did not want them to be adopted. She told her sisters that if they needed her children's help to do their work, they were welcome to ask for their help only, but to keep them as to adopt, no. She went on to say that her relatives were upset because she did not want them to adopt her children, but she did not give in.

More often, it appears, most young women bowed to the requests of older adults, especially older brothers. But again, as others have noted (e.g., Barnabas & Hezel, 1993; J.L. Fischer, 1970; M.C. Ward, 1989), adoption did not normally mean a significant break with the birth family.

Often children remained in the homestead or one nearby, and easily moved between the homes of many kin, whether or not these kin formally adopted them. In the past, children had many "parents" and most homes of their biological parents' kin were open to them for periods varying from a few days to many years. This appears less common in contemporary Pohnpei, although it does still occur.

Abortion

Nearly all informants insisted that no local medicines were used to bring on a late period or to terminate a known pregnancy. The literature also suggests that abortion may have been and may still be uncommon. For one thing, children were prized and in the past would have been fairly easily assimilated into the family and the clan, as everyone belongs to the clan of the mother. However, rather than there being no intentional abortions, the issue may be that people did not want to talk of such things, perhaps given the project's association with a Catholic organization and so many of the women being Catholic. Perhaps it was because abortion is illegal in Pohnpei. It was only after a significant period of association with me that anyone suggested that perhaps women might do something to terminate an unwanted pregnancy.

The idea that there might be local methods to terminate a pregnancy also came out in one woman's story of her first pregnancy, which was out of wedlock (this story was presented in Chapter 4). When her mother found out the woman was pregnant, the woman told her she wanted to get rid of the baby. The mother told her that "getting pregnant without a husband was wrong and shameful, but it would be a greater shame to get rid of the baby. The family would take care of her and the baby."

When methods were mentioned, most involved some kind of trauma that could lead to a spontaneous abortion. One involves very vigorous massage of the abdomen (womb). Another involved drinking a lot of very "sour" things, such as a large quantity of alcohol or soy sauce. The intention was to make the woman very sick so she would abort. Another method involved "jumping hard from a high place." But there are, or were, some local medicines that could be used. According to one woman, there is a set of medicines that comes in three types: "those to cleanse the womb, those to have babies, and those to get rid of babies." This woman claims that none of the techniques involve inserting anything into the vagina.

Legal medical abortions are not available on Pohnpei. However, women can get abortions overseas and apparently at least a few have done so. In at least one case this occurred while the woman was overseas attending university; others use a trip overseas as an opportunity to deal with an inopportune pregnancy.

Birth Control

When women introduced the topic of birth control they generally used the term *birth control* more often than phrases such as *family planning*, although some also talked in terms of spacing their children. Even when they were speaking in their own language they used the English language phrase.

According to the older women from all groups, the only kinds of birth control they ever used were abstinence and, for a few, ritualized burial of the placenta. The required period of abstinence varied from one month to one year and the amount of time varied by respondent rather than cultural group; thus, women within the same cultural group sometimes reported different lengths of time.

Ritualized burial of the placenta was described by a small number of women; the youngest was in her late 20s. The way the placenta is buried is associated with such things as the length of time between pregnancies and the total number of pregnancies. These women told us that if the placenta was buried deep, the time to the next pregnancy would be long. If the burial was shallow, it would not be long before the woman got pregnant again. If they wanted many babies they buried it shallow. If they wanted few babies or more space in between them, they buried it deep. The burial may or may not have been accompanied by ritual or magical talk, a chant, or a spell.

Some describe the use of birth control as more common among younger women, in particular working women. One woman's comments suggested that working women feel a greater need to space their children because of their need to work and that they are aware of the economic issues associated with having children, especially a large family. First, for example, women do not get paid maternity leave. To maintain their incomes and their jobs, they return to work as soon as possible after a birth. This can be within a month. Normally women in government employment are allowed a month of leave. If they have accumulated holiday or sick leave, they use that. Otherwise the leave is unpaid. In some departments, the women can negotiate for an advance on their leave. In the private sector the leave is generally unpaid. These women also recognize other economic factors, such as the need to pay school fees for each new child, fees that may eventually include college and university fees. These women say that people today also want to have nice houses and nice things in their houses, and that all of these things cost money. Women take such things into consideration when they consider birth control.

"In 1965 (31 years ago) the then U.S. Secretary of the Interior issued a directive mandating the establishment of Family Planning Programs throughout its territories, including the former Trust Territory of the Pacific Islands (TTPI)" (Pretrick, 1997, p. 111). Although many local leaders were not initially receptive to the idea of family planning, it was well instituted in all the states of FSM by 1983 (Pretrick, 1997). At this point "a wide range of contraceptives became available at very low cost" (Pretrick, 1997, p. 112). In many cases they are free of charge.

According to some government informants, birth control is reasonably well accepted in Pohnpei and FSM. Dr. Eliuel Pretrick, Secretary of Health for FSM, reports that in 1995 the "contraceptive prevalence rate was 49.9%. If men practicing family planning (using condoms) were counted, this contraceptive prevalence rate increases to more than 60%" for FSM as a whole (Pretrick, 1997, p. 112) (however, see Chapter 2). In terms of Pohnpei these figures must be considered in the context of its large Roman Catholic population (which may or may not affect contraception use) and are, therefore, probably somewhat lower. However, data for Pohnpei in the last few years was unavailable at the time of this report.

In Pohnpei, in addition to abstinence and the rhythm method,[5] a wide range of options are available, including "all kinds of pills," "injectables" (depo provera), the Norplant implant, loops, condoms, and foams. The only form not available is the diaphragm, in part because it has never been a popular option. According to these people, the most popular are pills and the Norplant implant. Although foams and creams are not popular in Pohnpei, they are popular, according to these people, on Kosrae. The reasons for differences in preference are not clear. One woman suggested that women may prefer forms that do not directly involve touching their "private properties," their genitals.

According to the *Digest of Health Statistics 1990* (Government of the Federated States of Micronesia, 1990), for the period 1986–1989, the most popular form of birth control among "new acceptors" was the pill followed by the IUD (Table 6.1).

Although older women do not report using birth control (see Chapter 2 for related information on fertilty), many are not adverse to it. For example, one woman, now in her 60s, sent one of her daughters to get the "injection" after the birth of her fourth child because the daughter had such a hard time after each birth, namely pain and abdominal cramps.[6] The fact that this woman suggested the injection may be related to her negative associations with her tubal ligation. This woman was told she had a lump or mass in her abdomen and was sent to the hospital for surgery shortly after the birth of her tenth child. She said

Table 6.1
Family Planning: New Acceptors by Method 1986–1989

| | Year | | | |
Method	1986	1987	1988	1989
Pill	245	170	215	93
IUD	134	101	104	33
Condom	74	83	85	95
Tubal-ligation	81	40	58	50
Vasectomy	5	1	1	2
Hysterectomy	3	1	4	7
Rhythm	3	3	1	2
Depo	0	0	0	291
Total	545	399	468	573

Adapted from Government of the Federated States of Micronesia (1990). Digest of Health Statistics 1990. Pohnpei, FSM: Government of the Federated States of Micronesia Department of Human Resources Medical and Vital Statistics Office.

all that was done was a tubal ligation. Now, many years later, she associates some of her current health problems with this surgery.

This woman is not the only one who associates tubal ligation with health problems that range from general poor health to specific aches and pains. In another interview the woman asked me to explain tubal ligation, the loop, and the implant, and the advantages of each. It soon became evident that what she really wanted to know was whether her tubal ligation was associated with a particular health problem she was having now, nearly 20 years after the surgery.

NOTES

1. Hezel (personal communication, July 1999) says Ashby's translation for *pilen dihdi* is incorrect. It translates as "breast milk," not "watery breast."

2. L. Englberger is conducting nutritional analyses of the *karat* banana and other traditional foods as part of her doctoral research on Vitamin A deficiency in FSM.

3. J.L. Fischer (1970) suggests that the introduction of bottle-feeding may have facilitated adoption at an early age. People believed that if a child was adopted early it would have a better relationship with the adoptive parents.

4. The June 1999 issue of *Pacific Islands Monthly* published an article on external adoptions in the Marshall Islands called "Adoptions Are Out of Control in the Marshalls." This article raises some concerns about the number of adoptions by people living off-island, presumably non-Marshallese, the ease with which they occur, and controversies about the kinds of restrictions that can be imposed by the U.S. Immigration and Naturalization Service. The number of such adoptions is considerably fewer in Pohnpei. Nevertheless people are beginning to raise concerns about nonlineage formal adoptions for reasons other than thinking they are evidence of the moral decay of society.

5. One conversation I had with a Pohnpeian woman suggested that when some women talk about abstinence, they may also be referring to the rhythm method. Although it was not completely clear, and we were interrupted before I could find out, she may have included it with abstinence because the method involves a period of abstinence during the month.

6. Although the description of the daughter's problems focused on physical symptoms, the mother's description suggested that psychological symptoms may also have been involved.

Chapter 7

Menopause

Several of the older women have stopped menstruating (see Table 2.5). The earliest reported age was 38 and the oldest 58, with most in their 40s and 50s. Most of these women told us that they were not surprised when they stopped, that their friends had told them they would. This appears to be something that, at least in the past, only mature women talked about. Thus these women told us that they became aware that women stop menstruating, and that this was normal, only as they neared the time of menopause. Younger women (i.e., younger than 50) seemed more aware of menopause than women may have been in the past. One woman in her 40s told us she had learned about it in school.

Menopause was not something the older women could elaborate on. Women get old and eventually just stop having periods: it is normal and it happens—end of story. It is simply "what God has planned." They did have some ideas about when this should happen, however. Some women said that women stopped in their 50s, but that it varied from one woman to another. On the other hand, some women talked about what is normal by first discussing what they saw as abnormal or unusual. For example, the woman who stopped in her late 30s thought that was too early and had been concerned about it. A woman in her 40s who described a recent "abnormal" bleeding episode (she bled for several weeks) asked if this could be a sign that she was reaching menopause. She said she had gone to a local healer, who told her, "No, it can't be. It is too early." Obviously the woman was not totally convinced and

that is why she asked me. It was also clear that she was concerned that
if it was menopause, it was too early and signaled that something was
wrong with her.[1]

The idea that the 40s were a bit young for menopause came up in
other contexts as well. For example, a similar situation to the one above
occurred during a period of observation in one of the outpatient clinics.
The woman had come in because she was having "heavy periods." When
I asked the woman's age the doctor said, "She is 48. She is nearing
menopause age." This comment suggests that doctors also may see the
40s as young for menopause. I did not have an opportunity to ask what
the doctor thought was "the" age for menopause, but some women in
the community told me they thought 50 was "normal."

SIGNS AND SYMPTOMS

Few women reported any kinds of signs or symptoms other than
changes in their menstrual flow (both periods with heavy bleeding and
periods with decreased bleeding) and the cessation of their periods. For
two of the women, their periods simply stopped. Women generally did
not talk about erratic or irregular periods. Only one woman talked about
disturbing mood changes during this phase of her life. One woman suggested that Pohnpeian women might have fewer symptoms during menopause because of their diet.

NO OBVIOUS STATUS OR ROLE CHANGE

I was not able to get women to elaborate on life differences after
menopause. My impression is that none is linked specifically to menopause. Essentially what they told me was, "You have periods for a while
and then you don't." As noted above, it is considered no big deal—it
happens and it's normal. Because menstrual status is considered private
and personal, it is possible that it is not linked to status or role changes
in later life, as in some other societies. Nevertheless, this may be a topic
worthy of further investigation using slightly different questioning
strategies.

GETTING OLDER

Women did talk about some changes that occurred as women age,
although they were not necessarily directly related to menopause. They
talked about losing or thinning pubic hair. They talked about a decrease
in their libido; in fact, they talked about getting too old for sex or it

being unseemly for older women to have sex. In one interview the women talked about increased discomfort during intercourse as a result of a decrease in vaginal secretions. On the other hand, one woman said that although "her desire for sex is no longer that strong," it is the desire for sex that "keeps people strong."

> It [sex] moves our whole system such as "blood, muscles, nerves, bones, everything." That is why they believe that sex does have a good effect on our health. It keeps a person going healthy. Without that desire, people feel weak and old. However, this also depends on each individual. Some people, the older they get, their libido enhanced. Unfortunately, people don't think it is normal when some people experience this way. They say that they are *sengeu* or *dirkihla sengeu*, which is a term they used for people who are too sexually active or sex maniac (maybe?). She said that some people, once they reach old age, they are not that active in sex anymore, however, others she said . . . are more sexually active even though they are old.

This set of comments was followed by some "sexual joking" among the interview participants about the sexuality of older people from different parts of Pohnpei and Micronesia. Then the second woman involved in the interview returned to the topic of decreased libido and comfort level during sex. She also talked about how young people do not expect older people to be sexually active.

> Especially with our children, they expect that when we reach old age, we should not be sexually active anymore. (We also laughed when she said, "Oooh, it is not good anymore.") The children might feel embarrassed to know their mother or father is still sexually active even when they are considered to be old. Our custom is also shying away from this kind of thing. But the other lady said that there shouldn't be any shame about this because this is part of life and this is what makes people happy and strong.

During one of the interviews one of the older women asked why "some women cannot walk straight up. They are bent forward when they walk instead of walking straight and tall." We asked the woman why she thought this was before we gave our idea. She thought it was "nerves," and in her opinion, these were "women who abused themselves both sexually and through hard labor." I suggested that another possible explanation was that they had something called osteoporosis from a lack of calcium in their diet. That led to a discussion of the kinds of food that are high in calcium.

A couple of the older women suggested that as people age they once again become like children, that this is part of the natural cycle of life. "She also said that as people get older, they begin to behave more or less like children again. For example, the women stop their menstruation periods, they start to lose the hair at their private areas (loud laugh) . . . eh?"

MENOPAUSE INTO THE FUTURE

Although we asked about menopause and probed for some details about it, the women seemed to have little to offer on the subject, perhaps because such discussions occurred late in the interviews, or perhaps because they have little to say on the topic at this point. In terms of these data, menopause does not appear to be a marked category in Pohnpei, socially or in terms of health. Older women were aware of it, even if they had not yet stopped menstruating. Some younger women were also aware that older women stop menstruating. As long as women associated this break in their menstrual pattern as something normal and natural, they weren't concerned about it. Menstruation simply ceases when women achieve a certain age; it is something that just happens. It is normal and natural.

Because Pohnpei appears to be a case where menopause is not associated with so many of the things (symptoms, role changes, etc.) seen in Western societies, it could provide an opportunity for comparative studies. Is the lack of elaboration social, physical, or some combination? Were we just not able to obtain the necessary information? Did we ask the right questions? In the future, will understanding of and attitudes toward menopause change in the modern social and medical context? Will changes in lifestyle and diet affect the menopausal experience? So many other areas of women's menstrual and reproductive lives have changed in Pohnpei. Will this also change?

NOTE

1. As with all women who raised questions associated with concerns about their health, the woman was asked what she thought before I shared "what the scientists say." The woman was then advised to see a doctor if her description suggested something worthy of further investigation or if such a consultation would relieve her anxiety. Most of the questions were simply requests for explanations about normal things, such as the normal age for menopause. On the other hand, very often it became clear that the women were just seeking a second opinion. Some had already been to a doctor.

Chapter 8

In the Context of Change

Culture is in a constant process of change. The culture of Pohnpei today is in an unusual state of cultural flux, largely because of outside influences. Pohnpei is responding not only to issues associated with its relationship with the United States and the resulting changes in the sociopolitical and economic environment, but also to other global changes in all these areas. Two areas undergoing particular change are daily life and health and health care. Again, many of the changes are the result of outside influences, including exposure to other ideas about health, illness, and healing.

Menstruation, pregnancy, and birthing are important aspects of women's lives; they help identify them as women. Having children, naturally or through adoption, is a social expectation, one that helps assure a woman's identity and her place in her social world. These experiences and what they mean are undergoing many fundamental changes, however. Women are having fewer children and producing them in ways and in contexts that are different from the past. Women are taking on expanded roles, and many now work outside the family, not only out of necessity, but also because they want to, and see the opportunity to work and earn a wage as a right. These changes are both the product of and the explanation for changes in the family in Pohnpei.

In nearly all the interviews the talk turned to changes in Pohnpeian society and in the lives of Pohnpeians, particularly women and families. In some cases this was a response to questions about how age at menarche and first pregnancy might have changed. Often the women initiated such talk. Almost any topic could stimulate talk about how things have changed, and they returned to the topic time and time again. In almost all interviews (across cultural groups), especially with the older women (40 and above), this was a closing theme and was often in response to closing questions like, "Is there anything we have not talked about that you think we should know?"

The material presented in the earlier sections suggests that there have been many changes in relation to menstruation and childbirth, especially over the last 50 years or so. The following are just some of these changes:

- More young women know about menstruation before it happens, so it is a less traumatic event than in the past.
- There is a greater openness in talking about women's things such as menstruation.
- Age at menarche appears to be younger, yet menarche is no longer viewed as a sign of reproductive readiness.
- The number of pregnancies and the size of completed families have decreased and will probably continue to decrease.
- More women are planning their families and use modern contraception resources to do so.
- Education and wage employment probably have a significant influence on family planning decisions.
- A large family is no longer automatically viewed as a sign of economically, socially, psychologically, and morally sound behavior or as an advantage to the family.
- Not only is the structure of the family changing, but there are also changes in the social and economic expectations for the family and family members. There are also inter- and intrafamily changes that affect women's experiences, particularly their experiences of pregnancy and childbirth.
- Fewer women are following traditional birthing practices or believe in the old beliefs, and some young women are not even aware of many of them.
- Pregnancy and giving birth are now often conceptualized using primarily a Western biomedical framework, rather than a uniquely Pohnpeian one.
- Yet local medicine is still part of pregnancy and birthing, even when it is neither recognized nor approved by people within the medical system or some of the women themselves.
- Today nearly all deliveries occur at the hospital, and it has become an event that many women share only with hospital staff.
- The support system during the early postpartum period is now available for only a short period of time, if at all.

- New mothers are no longer treated like a queen and indulged for a significant period of time.
- Pregnancy, childbirth, and becoming a mother have changed from an interpersonal and social event that binds female kin together and enhances a young woman's claim to adult status to a rather individual event that takes place in a context of nonkin and focuses on the biomechanics of pregnancy, labor, and delivery.
- Pregnancy and childbirth are less physically dangerous than in the past, but the risk of mental health problems among young mothers may be increasing.
- Breast-feeding is replacing bottle-feeding as the most prestigious way to nourish an infant.
- Although the legitimization of a pregnancy has always been bound up with such things as age and marital status, age has acquired a special importance. Legitimization in terms of age has become an issue because people have adopted Western standards for judging the propriety of a pregnancy, and adolescence has been extended to include all the teen years.
- Adoption and fosterage are less common and more formal, so adoption is no longer readily available as an adaptive (and socially accepted) strategy for young and/or unwed mothers who are not quite ready to assume a more adult role.
- Many young women may not be well prepared to take on the role of mother because they increasingly have less and less mothering experience as children or adolescents.
- There are breaks in women's traditional knowledge about these events because of changes in the family and factors such as a longer time in the educational system. The educational system often takes young women away from the family context for significant periods of time during a period when much of this knowledge is acquired experientially through interaction with mothers, children, and pregnant relatives and friends.
- On the other hand, mothers and daughters may, in many cases, be more open to talking about such things, but often such talk focuses on ideas and concepts acquired through interaction with Western-oriented knowledge systems: school and the medical system.

Although each of these points is worthy of more detailed exploration, this section focuses more on the concerns women raised in the interviews that they wanted included.

SOCIAL CHANGE AND MORAL AND PHYSICAL DECAY

The women feel, justly so, that there have been major, even dramatic, changes within their lifetimes. They talk with amazement about these dramatic changes, but not always in terms of the good they may have brought to people's lives, although the women certainly do that as well. Much of the talk might be described as discussions of the "moral decay" of society, particularly among young people, that is the result of all these changes. Some women also talked about a kind of "physical decay" among women today. In some cases the same explanations are used, often at the same time, for things that are both good and bad, particularly in the area of changes in women's bodies. It is important to note that *moral decay* and *physical decay* are my terms, not theirs, but I think they cover the essence of what these women said, and what they asked me to include.

These comments also reflect the opinions of some of the others interviewed formally or informally during the course of this project. Although the comments probably better reflect the perspectives of the older generations, some young people seemed to have a similar perspective. Others embrace modern life and want things to change even more rapidly—or at least for the moment they do. They may change their minds one day.

Talk about the decay of society is not new. As M.C. Ward noted more than ten years ago:

> Sometimes Westerners naively refer to places such as Micronesia as "primitive" or simple. Some times the Pohnpeians blame their current problems on U.S. colonialism. Most of the time Westerners and Pohnpeians alike tell anthropologists that the past was a golden time of rich rituals and reverence for custom, when life's meanings were clear and all children respected their elders. None of these folk beliefs are true. (M.C. Ward, 1989, p. 43)

Nor are such sentiments specific to Pohnpei. Most societies at one time or another talk of a "golden age" when all was right with the world, an age that probably exists only in people's minds. Such talk takes on a special flavor in regard to Pohnpei, however, and in the process it highlights the kinds of things people consider important, what they think makes life worth living.

MORAL DECAY

According to one woman, many traditional practices were

> a way of enforcing respect during those days. Nowadays, since we are becoming Christians we no longer believe in those old customs, but they feel so strange when they observe kids nowadays who do not care about being respectful. Children during those olden days were taught to be respect-

ful toward people to avoid any bad things from happening to them, and they actually respect those customs.

In terms of moral decay, people talk about how young people are not as respectful and responsible as they might have been in the past. They see young people as negatively influenced by exposure to things such as Western movies and television that openly depict sex and sexuality and violence. They feel that young people are more aware of things like sex at a much younger age than in their time, and that this encourages them to become sexually more active earlier than in the past. Even though there is evidence that women marry in their teens, and have for as long as many women can remember, and that young people were often sexually active in their "teen years," there is still a sense among many that such things are occurring earlier than in the past. Whether or not this is the case is unclear. Do they occur earlier, or is there a perception that they do because the standards have changed—in part because of exposure to the same Western (i.e., American) standards that many see as the cause instead of an effect?

All feel that young people are "freer" today. They do not think this freedom is necessarily bad. In many ways they feel it is good: young people go off to school, become educated, and bring knowledge back to their community; they have a stronger say in decisions such as whom they will marry and how many children they will have. But this freedom may not have come with the same sense of responsibility. Although outside influences (e.g., the Americanization of Micronesia) must account for some of the change, women more often blamed the parents of the wayward young and did so more quickly. They cited not so much the effect of Americanization or Westernization as something within the character of contemporary young Pohnpeians and, in some cases, the loss or deterioration of the Pohnpeian family and culture.

What about the young girls nowadays—does she think they are younger when they start to have children?

She said the problem nowadays is that girls' mothers are very *saledek* or "free" these days. They seem not to worry of their kids' whereabouts nowadays. For example, the kids can go to parties and come back very late. Parents are not that strict any longer so that these kids tend to be getting into trouble. They are more involved in so many of these activities which involve both boys and girls.

She said that before, during her time, there were not that many types of intersexual activities which involve girls to participate without their parents. Today, there are alcohol and drugs to worry about that kids nowadays are taking. Before, only the *sakauen Pohnpei* that the older men and women drink.

Parents today, in many people's estimation, do not provide good role models. For instance, women go out to bars and leave young children alone at home, they do not show proper respect toward their brothers, and they do not discipline their children in ways that encourage responsibility. For them, freedom comes with responsibility. Young people are exercising their freedom, but not necessarily their responsibility.

These people are concerned about drugs and alcohol and intersex activities, especially those where there are no proper chaperones, and their effect on the lives and well-being of young people and their families. One woman said she did not remember there being many children with disabilities in the past, but now she sees many disabled children. She sees this increase as a direct result of drug and alcohol use in the community.[1] Implicit in such statements is that the "increase" (real or not) in the number of children with disabilities is not only the result of drug and alcohol use among young people, but also of their immoral behaviors, the result of both social and physical decay.

Although many of these women do not approve of people having sex at an earlier age (if in fact they are), they do not necessarily totally disapprove either. What they want is for young people to engage in responsible sexuality. They want them to enter into sexual relationships well aware of the potential consequences of their actions, namely pregnancy. (Only people involved in government and nongovernment health and social programs, and those who are highly educated mentioned sexually transmitted diseases as a consequence.) They want young people to realize that if the girl gets pregnant, her life will be greatly affected. She will generally have to withdraw from school to care for the child. She will lose some of her freedom. As already noted, today many parents are unwilling or unable to take on the care of their child's child, whether or not the young mother was married. Women more often work outside of the home. They are no longer "stay at home" grandmothers who can or will take care of new additions to the family. In many cases, the young mother's mother may not be available to help her through childbirth or with the care of her infant. They may live on different islands or in different parts of the world.

One of the consequences of parents not being willing or able to care for their unwed daughter's child is that some children are being given up for adoption to people outside of the lineage. As we were closing an interview with two of the oldest Pohnpeian women, they told me there was something they wanted me to know and note in my report. They said that young women today are giving their children away in adoption. They obviously saw this as a bad thing.

I asked, "Is this different than the kind of sharing of children people did in the past?" They answered, "Yes." What they were talking about was formalized, legal adoptions, particularly outside of the lineage. If I understood these and other women correctly, they saw this as evidence of this moral decay I have mentioned. These young women were "throwing away" their children to strangers (other Micronesians or Westerners). This was not an issue of temporary, or even semipermanent, foster care in which the woman would still be a part of the child's life. In this kind of adoption, the children are permanently lost to the girl, her family, and the lineage. The women who talked about such things simply could not understand how a girl could give away her child in such a permanent way.

Older people also want the young to engage in responsible sexuality because they are concerned about the reputations of these young people and how these reflect on the entire family. Young women with reputations as "wild girls" are viewed as not likely to marry well. Perhaps more importantly, as the women noted so often in the interviews, a girl who gets pregnant out of wedlock brings shame to her family (at least temporarily). Her behavior is a reflection on the family. She alone is not responsible for her behavior, her whole family is, and her whole family must bear the responsibility and any long term repercussions of her inappropriate behavior.

An "inappropriate" pregnancy was viewed by many as evidence of bad parenting, not just youthful irresponsibility. Parents should have better control over their children and should teach them the "right" way to be a socially responsible person. As in other areas of the Pacific, the issue here is, I believe, not so much that young people should not engage in sexual relations, but that they do so responsibly. For one thing, they should not get caught (see also Falgout, 1993).

In fact, as Falgout (1993, p. 132) and others point out, at least in the past, if not today, secret sexual liaisons negotiated through an intermediary were "considered a normal and exciting part of Pohnpei life." They were considered shameful only if they became public knowledge. Once pregnant, a girl cannot deny having been sexually active. In addition, they should not engage in indiscriminant sexual behavior, or sex for the sake of sex. Rather, as one informant suggests, becoming involved with someone sexually can be part of the search for a future mate, and sometimes, this means that ultimately a young person might have several partners before choosing one. Such behavior might be more acceptable if conducted discreetly, and in some cases with the approval of the family, by young people who are sexually mature[2] and ready to accept and assume adult roles (see also the next section). It would still not be publicly condoned, but it would, nevertheless, be more acceptable. On the other hand, standards may be changing for all the reasons cited earlier.

There is in the data on Pohnpei, in the literature and the interviews, a sense that the values used to judge people's behavior have also changed. In particular I refer to changes in attitudes toward sex, sexuality, and sex among the unmarried. In some cases this seems to reflect a strong move toward fundamental Christian values or an increase in conservatism. This may not accurately reflect the overarching values of contemporary Pohnpei because so many of the women we interviewed were Catholic and most saw us as associated with Catholicism. Nevertheless, discussions in other contexts suggest that there is a special kind of conservatism in Pohnpei, one that may reflect not only religion and culture but also a response to rapid cultural change and concerns about losing local culture. This is akin to what Eisenbruch (1992) calls "cultural bereavement." It is not, as Eisenbruch notes, some kind of pathology, but a normal response to cultural change.

Ideals and Cultural Change

M.C. Ward talks about issues such as sex, pregnancy, and adoption in her book *Nest in the Wind: Adventures in Anthropology on a Tropical Island*. Much of her information is consistent with that acquired during this study.

> There is a Pohnpeian word meaning "to pick too young," which refers to the appropriate age for intercourse to begin. The ages customarily mentioned are lower than most Westerners find comfortable. The lower limit of sexual activity for girls was variously placed at eleven to fourteen years of age, certainly by fifteen to nineteen for conservative folk. It is generally assumed that intercourse is appropriate if a girl has started to menstruate and is not exposed to any situation that would harm her, emotionally or physically. Boys usually begin their sexual lives later than girls as their bodies are believed to mature more slowly.
>
> The next question foreigners usually ask is, "But what if she gets pregnant?" The answer is incredibly simple. In Pohnpei, children are highly valued. Illegitimacy is not even a word. Children automatically belong to their mother's clan. So they have a social affiliation that only marriage gives in U.S. society. Children will have many males and females in their extended family to love and care for them. The man who weds their mother is considered their father. In fact, pregnancy is the reason a couple will regularize their union and settle down. A woman may select a mate

during or even after her first pregnancy. The practice of adoption serves to reduce the pressures of unwanted pregnancy. Obviously, a century and a half of exuberant contact between islanders with their easy sexual mores and foreigners resulted in babies. All of them absorbed easily into their clans and families.

The outstanding characteristic of the value system of family life on Pohnpei is the warm practicality. It sounds so obvious and trite to say that children should be highly valued or that sexual activities should be frequent, discrete, mutually satisfactory to both partners, and harmful to no one, but those values are at the center of Pohnpeian culture. (M.C. Ward, 1989, p. 43)

As this report indicates, M.C. Ward's comments seem to better reflect a time in the recent past—her fieldwork took place in the 1970s—and perhaps, a more distant past. Because much of the current research took place in and around Kolonia, the urban center, it may reflect the values and attitudes of only a segment of Pohnpei's population. More research in the rural communities and the outer islands might indicate more remnants of the past, as a few informants have suggested.

In the past, according to the literature and some informants involved in this research, young people began to engage in sexual activity at a fairly young age, after menarche but before marriage. This would mean, if our data on menarche, first pregnancy, and age at marriage are reasonably accurate, that women might begin to have sex in their midteens but not become pregnant or marry until their late teens or early 20s. Pregnancy was often used as a reason for a marriage, but women did have children out of wedlock who were absorbed into the lineage through adoption or fosterage. Sometimes a woman had more than one child before she and/or her family decided it was time for her to marry. She might marry the biological father of her child or children, but if she did not, her husband would accept any child in her womb or any child living with her as his own.

This portrait may still reflect today's reality, but it does not reflect what is viewed as ideal or proper in modern Pohnpeian society, at least not in the view of the people with whom I talked. Today young people are expected to respect their elders and their opposite sex siblings, stay out of trouble, not use drugs and alcohol, complete their education, get a good job, and then marry someone of good repute from a highly respectable family with access to prized land and good titles. They are expected then, and only then, to have several children and to devote their lives to raising them to be socially and morally responsible adults.

All societies have their ideals, but more detailed research is needed to see just how modern Pohnpeian society might actually vary from this ideal. There certainly are young women getting pregnant in their teens, but is this truly greater than in the past? There certainly are women getting pregnant without being married, but again, is this truly more common than in the past? The actual numbers are most certainly greater—the population of Pohnpei has increased dramatically—but are the numbers relatively greater? This research raises this question but the data are insufficient to answer it with any level of confidence. More research, research that more directly addresses such questions, is needed.

Physical Decay

Although women often explained the earlier age at menarche as the product of girls being healthier today than in the past, they also talked about young women as less healthy than in the past. Young women were described as bigger—taller and heavier—than in the past, and they were described as having poor diets, eating chips and drinking sodas. As a result, they were often under- or malnourished, and this had implications for their health and the health of their unborn children. Some women believe there are more serious diseases among contemporary women. For example some felt that cancer, particularly uterine or cervical cancer, was a more common health problem now than in the past. These women explained this, at least in part, by the decreased use of traditional herbal remedies, especially those designed to maintain a woman's health by keeping her womb healthy and clean.

How do we reconcile this apparent paradox? Women and girls (as general categories) cannot be more healthy and less healthy at the same time. On the one hand the explanation may be that until recently, for example during the young women's childhoods, children's diets were better than in the distant past, particularly during the war years, but may have deteriorated in more recent years. This is within the realm of the possible, but this seems unlikely, considering the incidence of lifestyle- and dietary-related diseases, such as diabetes and cardiovascular disease, among Pacific Islander populations. Furthermore, the evidence in Demory's (1976) study on the economics of political status rivalry and its effects on the nutrition and health of young children suggests that undernutrition has at least a 25-year history, one that would include many of the young people they are talking about. Poor nutrition is not necessarily associated with smaller stature. Thus it is possible that girls can be both improperly nourished and heavier or bigger than in the past, and they can be healthy in some ways but not in others. For example, young people may have fewer serious, life-threatening, infectious diseases and still be at risk for other illnesses associated with lifestyle—ones that might not become apparent until they are older. They may have fewer health problems, or appear to have fewer problems, but the ones they have may place their children at risk.

One of the women told us that in the period after the war when many imported foods were first being introduced, parents often gave their limited supply of imported foods (e.g., rice, canned goods, and sweets) to their children whereas they ate traditional foods (e.g., yams and fresh fish). These parents thought they were doing something good for their children. Only now do they realize that what they thought was the second-rate diet may have been the more healthful one. There is a very similar scenario in terms of bottle-feeding and breast-feeding. Women who in the past breast-fed their children because they did not have access to bottles and formula or could not afford them now realize that their children may have been given the better option, although they did not think so at the time. The standards have changed and so have the health issues. For some, this is a kind of physical decay.

CHANGE AND OTHER RELATED THINGS

All of the talk about change did not occur within the context of discussions easily labeled as about moral or physical decay, and some are not directly related to women's reproductive health. Some just simply dealt with the way some things have changed. Many reflect issues the women wanted raised. All of these points raise more questions than they answer.

Changing Female Bodies

In addition to discussions about the physical health of young people as compared with the health of older women, people also talked about something that might be described as changes in the shape of female bodies. First, young women were described as taller and heavier than women in the past. They were described as having larger and fuller breasts, which, as noted earlier, one woman associated with all the additives in processed foods. Older women are described by some of the women as having nicer figures, particularly flatter stomachs, compared with younger women, despite the fact that they had more children. Whether this reflects a traditional ideal of female shape and beauty or the influence of exposure to Western images of the ideal shape is unclear. In one conversation a women indicated that she thought lightly colored skin and a slim figure like mine were preferable to her more richly hued color and robust figure. Several young women's opinions offered in informal situations suggested that their ideals were affected by the images of women they see in Western movies and magazines. And how much has the image of the ideal shape been influenced by public health educational messages about the relationship between obesity and problems such as diabetes and cardiovascular disease?

Pregnancy's Effect on Education

It is quite clear that people in the community, certainly in the urban and peri-urban areas, are increasingly deciding that an education through to high school, and often beyond, is important for young people today. Furthermore, as already noted, people regularly expressed concerns about how pregnancy interferes with a young woman's education and, therefore, her access to a good job in the future. The emphasis was on getting a good job, a good-paying job, not the effect education might have on her role as wife and mother in modern society, or how better-educated women tend to have healthier children. People talked about the pregnancy-related break in education as a problem, but the only solution they mentioned was finding ways to keep young women from getting pregnant. Although there appears to be some changes in regard to letting young mothers back into the school system, there was little discussion on how to get them back into the system or some alternate situation, such home- or village- or women's group–based literacy programs. When I mentioned the idea of a women's group–based literacy program using readings of interest to the young women to address a situation she described in a rural village, one woman seemed to think it was a rather novel idea.

Change in the Traditional Protective System

With cultural change have come changes in many other aspects of life. Women's lives are different in many ways than in the past, and the systems that protected women from harm in the past have also changed. In the past, a woman who was being abused or pressured into situations not of her liking (such as an arranged marriage with someone she did not like) had some options. They were not foolproof, but there were options.

For example, if she did not want to marry the boy or man chosen for her she could tell her parents. Sometimes the parents, especially if the girl was a favored child, would consider the girl's feelings, but that depended on the ultimate purpose of the marriage. The ultimate purpose of the marriage, such as keeping land in the family or cementing a critical social relationship, generally took precedence over the girl's wishes. For many things, such as difficulties with her husband, a woman could go talk to her mother or sometimes even her mother-in-law. Although these women would probably tell her to keep quiet about the problem so she would not bring shame to the family, they could intervene on her behalf or help her devise a strategy to deal with the situation.

> Even in those days the women, her complaint is only supposed to be given to her mother and the mother of the boy. And it is not very safe if the fathers knew it because, you know they said that women can just talk— and nothing happened. But when the man also knows these things that are not well between the two parties, you know, things can be worse and they can not only talk but things can come up to, you know, fighting. So we are told not to talk. When there is something happening in the family women keep their mouths shut. Certainly don't create more frictions. Just let the lady who is chosen to be the mother of the clan to talk. 'Cause she is the only power. With the two families.

This "mother of the clan" (*limesekedil*) was described as the ultimate advocate of Pohnpeian women. Despite descriptions of men as the ultimate power and authority in Pohnpeian society, the *limesekedil* was described as having an even higher level of power and authority. One woman told us that this woman was so powerful, she could stop a man with a gun. If she told this man to put the gun down, he would put it down. Men had, and continue to have, power and authority in many domains—perhaps in contemporary Pohnpei they have even more power and authority than in the past in some areas—but women's power was, and for many still is, a kind of ultimate power.

Barnabas and Hezel (1993) also note that minor disputes within families were generally resolved by the parents. More serious matters could be taken to the maternal uncle, *uhlap*, or the maternal aunt. Disputes between distant members of the lineage and those between spouses could be taken to the lineage head (*mesenihn*) or the senior woman of the lineage (*limesekedil*).

According to women involved in this study, especially those from matrilineal groups, women could expect their brothers to come to their aid, an expectation many continue to have. As already noted, the bond between brothers and sisters is very powerful in Micronesia. It is a relationship tied together with reciprocal rights and responsibilities. Thus a woman could expect her brothers to protect her from a husband's abusive behavior. She could also expect her brothers to punish her if, in any way, she brought shame to the family. Brothers would often not be the first people women would go to, however. As the woman above noted, violence became a real possibility when men became involved; young men were, after all, warriors whose job it was to protect the family and the family's land.

The traditional protective system, namely the family, is not as readily available as it once was, particularly in the more urban area in and around Kolonia. Women in Kolonia often do not live as close to female kin and brothers as they once did; they may not even live in or near the home of their mother-in-law. With the nuclearization of the modern family, the nature of familial relationships has changed (for further details on such changes see Barnabas & Hezel, 1993). Husbands and wives live together in a relatively more isolated life; they rely on each other more than in the past and they rely on each other in different ways. Male and female roles, particularly within the nuclear family, have undergone some critical transformations, ones that sometimes leave women more vulnerable than in the past. The traditional protective network does not function in the same way, or it may not work as smoothly as it once did. There is often no family immediately available to intercede or to mediate disputes.

This does not mean that these networks and protective systems no longer exist; they do, but in a modified form. Today women are increasingly likely to turn to friends outside of the family and to the church and social services for assistance. When domestic violence happens, the police are more likely to become involved than in the past. Before, this would have been a family, lineage, or even clan issue; it would have been taken care of internally. There appears to be a transformation from a reliance on family to a reliance on the self or social services, something seen in other populations as well (see for example Fitzgerald et al., 1998).

The Changing Nature of Marriage

As noted earlier, people may engage in a series of clandestine sexual relationships before settling into a long-term relationship. They may also be involved in a sequence of serious relationships ("marriages") in which the couple live together for varying periods of time. A couple may even have several children before they and their families decide to formalize the relationship. As Falgout (1993) notes:

> For all the importance placed upon marriage in traditional Pohnpei, early marriages are very fragile. Divorce—or "unravelling the knot" of marriage—is rather easy for young couples; it can be instigated by either party and simply involves their separating and returning to their respective family residences. After a couple has lived together for a long period of

time and has given birth to their own children; however, their union is expected to be lasting and divorce is much less acceptable. (Falgout, 1993, p. 136)

Like the women in this study, Falgout (1993) discusses how, as a result of contact with other cultures, marriage and divorce practices in Pohnpei have undergone many changes over the years. Falgout (1993, p. 128) notes that although these practices have come to look more Western and formal church sanctioned marriages are more common and divorce more difficult, "the motivations for marriage remain decidedly Pohnpei."

In the past, families arranged most marriages, whether or not they were formalized in any way. The arrangements might even be made when women were infants. Marriage in those days was tied to economic and social concerns, especially to keeping land and titles within the family, cementing relations between two families, and enhancing status—and these things continue to be important for many people. Although some women would be betrothed to men they knew, men they had known all their lives because they lived near one another, particularly on the outer islands, others never even saw their prospective husbands before the "wedding." This wedding might entail the ritual exchange of a small token of respect, such as a drinking coconut or a stalk of sugar cane, between the prospective husband and his family and the woman's family (Falgout, 1993). If the families considered the marriage agreeable, the couple moved in together. In the past they might have moved into the household compound of the woman's family. More recently, the couple is more likely to move in with the man's family. However, as noted in chapter 2 (see also Falgout, 1993; Barnabas & Hezel, 1993), residential patterns probably have always been quite flexible.

Many of these arranged marriages appear to have turned out well. They were long, happy, and productive in many ways, including producing many children. Others were fraught with problems, problems that might have begun even before the marriage took place.

One woman was asked: "How do you think things have changed since your mother's time, your time, and the young girl's time now? How are they different?" She said she would answer by making a comparison between 1950 and today. First she told us, "The good about being young and dating is that the girl and the boy learn to exchange ideas and learn the personalities of each other. And then they think, 'Oh, is this for my future or not.' In those days they just tell, you listen; last week they asked for you so next month you are going to get married with this."

She then went on to explain why the modern way was good by telling a tragic story about a girl who had been beaten when she tried to run away from an arranged marriage (Falgout, 1993 also notes that a woman could be beaten for refusing to marry a partner chosen for her).

> The girl, who did not want to marry this old man, ran away the night before the wedding. When she was found her brothers and father beat her quite severely with sticks. She had brought dishonor and disgrace to the family by running away so they punished her. She was subsequently married to the man and had 13 children with him. After the beating she had a lump near her collarbone which never went away. She later described this lump as "one of the long sufferings that I have, this part of me used to be, I used to having pain daily." Many years later, she went to a local healer because of pain in this area. The healer gave her massage and told her she needed to go to the hospital but she did not want to go. The woman was afraid. She did not know how to explain how she got the lump. The healer told her to just ask the doctors to look at the lump, she did not have to tell her story about the beating. (Summary from transcript)

The message in this story is that in the past too many women suffered emotionally and physically because they were forced into marriages they did not want. The implication is that if girls have some choice, they will have a better life. This discussion went on to topics such as the changing purpose of marriage. In the past, marriages were often about land— acquiring land or maintaining access to plots of land.

Land is still important, but marriage as a means for acquiring land or access to it is of lesser importance today than in the past, or so some women say. Today women seem to feel that young women should have a choice about whom they marry without specific regard to whether or not they will acquire land. A couple of women told us that they approved of Western-style dating because they thought it provided young people with the chance to get to know one another's "minds" better so they could make a better, and perhaps happier, match. "That's why I say dating is good because they can, they can talk about things so they can see if their minds are the same, the balance of life that they would live in the future."

Others thought young people should choose their mate, but they were not comfortable with Western-style dating and thought young girls needed more supervision (see also Falgout, 1993). They wanted young people to meet in more controlled circumstances. No one advocated arranged marriages, but it was obvious that some parents play "matchmaker" or at least let their children know if they have some preference.

Knowledge about Women's Anatomy

It is unclear from the information collected during the interviews and in other contexts how much women know about their bodies or specifically female anatomy (a Western model or otherwise). There are indications that younger women may have a somewhat better understanding than older women because they may have learned about anatomy in school during science and health education programs. Some older women appeared quite knowledgeable. In other cases I was not sure. For example, I tried to answer one of the women's health questions with a pencil drawing of the female reproductive tract. Considering the kinds of questions she asked, she seemed comfortable with the drawing, but even at the time, I was wondering whether the drawing actually made any sense to the women before I explained it. I was not sure they had ever seen such a drawing before. This topic may be worthy of further investigation for a couple of reasons. First, it could tell us more about how women understand and visualize their bodies, and second, this knowledge might tell us more about the effectiveness of earlier educational programs and where differences in understandings might lead to misunderstandings of educational programs and health care instructions.

NOTES

1. Because there is so little data on disabilities in the Pacific, including Pohnpei, we cannot be sure there is an actual increase in the number of children with disabilities. Certainly improvements in the health care system have allowed some children with serious disabilities to survive. Special Education programs have also increased the identification and public recognition of these children, some of whom would have been kept hidden within the family compound in the past. For a review of the anthropological literature on disabilities, particularly that related to the Pacific, see for example Armstrong and Fitzgerald (Armstrong & Fitzgerald, 1996; Fitzgerald & Armstrong, 1993) and other Pacific-focused culture and disability-related publications by Fitzgerald and her colleagues (e.g., Anderson, Fitzgerald, Yee, & Wallace, 1996; Fitzgerald, 1993; Fitzgerald & Anderson, 1992; Fitzgerald & Barker, 1993; Fitzgerald, Yee, Goebert, & Okamoto, 1992). See also Marshall (1996).

2. As noted earlier and in the next section, menarche no longer appears to be considered a mark of sexual maturity, if it ever was.

Chapter 9

Conclusion

The purpose of this study was to explore the beliefs, practices, knowledge, thoughts, and experiences surrounding the reproductive lives of Micronesian women in Pohnpei, in particular menstruation, pregnancy, birthing, the postnatal period, and menopause. It was intended to be an initial exploration. Clearly some topics were addressed in more depth than others, and although others could have been addressed in more depth, their importance was not always fully realized until I began to put this book together. The project developed an additional purpose as it progressed. It became clear that many of the women became involved and fully supported the study because they wanted this kind of information archived. They have serious concerns that much of this information will die out in the "next few years" as young people do not seem very interested in the old ways. They are afraid that by the time these young women decide they want to know these things, no one will have the information to share with them. This does not mean that this is the definitive report—there are obvious gaps in many areas—but it is a first step toward preserving this kind of information.

Scholars will note that this report includes little in the way of analysis or interpretation. This is intentional. Given the women's desire to have the information "archived" and the promise to return something to them as soon as possible, and my need to organize the data in a useful way as one stage in analysis, I have chosen to concentrate primarily on a fairly straightforward presentation of the information. This format should allow people to engage in their own interpretations. This does not mean that I have not put forward some opinions, particularly in areas I see as especially problematic, but there is little of this in the book and what is there should be fairly obvious.

At this point the only conclusions I will offer are that the issues addressed in this book are important to women in Pohnpei and that cultural change has had an important effect on women's reproductive lives—some of it good and some not so good. I hope that the information presented here will allow people to make informed decisions in the future, whether these are personal decisions or decisions about social and health policy issues. Ideally it will help people identify areas that require attention and allow them to address them in a useful way. Ideally, it will help people put the Pohnpeian in Pohnpeian decision making in regard to women and women's health.

One thing is clear from this study: women's lives and their experiences as women are undergoing change (as they are in most societies). As we can see in Figure 9.1, biological, social, cultural, and psychological ex-

Figure 9.1
Interaction of Body, Mind, and Society

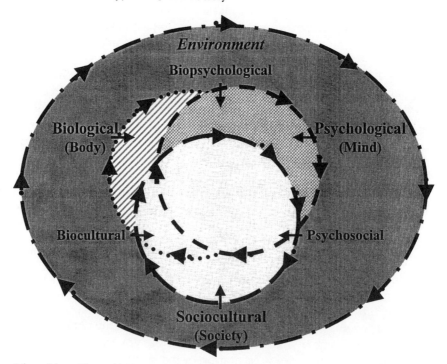

Adapted from Fitzgerald, *A Review and Critique of the Literature on Menstrual Beliefs*, 1984.

periences take place in context in an interactive way; change in any aspect evokes changes in the others. In this case, Western, in particular American, influences have had a significant effect on these experiences and the perceptions of these experiences. Women today are in many ways healthier and have more knowledge about particular aspects of their lives, and fewer women and children die in the perinatal period. At the same time, all is not good. Women today have other health concerns and needs. Some of these are being addressed well; others are not. In the future there will be new health concerns, in part as the result of cultural change and in part because of changes in the socioeconomic and political situation in Pohnpei and FSM. Although little evidence surfaced of significant mental health problems in the postnatal period—one of the questions this study sought to address—there is evidence that many of the changes in Pohnpei and in women's lives place them at greater risk for such problems. The decrease, or at least changes, in family support during pregnancy, birthing, and the postnatal period place many young women at increased risk. Can the health system, particularly given current funding and access to needed goods and services, address these needs adequately? Should they? If so, how can they do so in a way that acknowledges that any change will evoke other, often unexpected, changes?

I am not advocating a return to the past, particularly not some "golden age" that exists only in people's minds. But I do suggest that information about the past (the kind of information presented here) and the identified strengths of the past be considered in health care and social decision making. I do advocate using the whispers of the mothers to help make informed decisions that keep Pohnpei and Pohnpeian women's lives Pohnpeian. If this is to occur, there is a need for more studies of this kind, ones in which women get to have their say, to have their voices heard—in all their complexity and diversity. If we listen hard enough, we can hear the whispers of the mothers both young and old. If we listen hard enough, we just might learn something.

References

Ahlburg, D.A. (1996). Demographic and social change in the island nations of the Pacific (Asia-Pacific Population Research Report). Honolulu: East-West Center Program on Population.

American Psychiatric Association. (1994). *Diagnostic and statistical manual of mental disorders* (4th ed.). Washington, DC: American Psychiatric Association.

Anderson, D.D., Fitzgerald, M.H., Yee, H.K.M., & Wallace, G.L. (1996). Planning rehabilitation services for rural and remote communities. In G.L. Wallace (Ed.), *Adult aphasia rehabilitation* (pp. 325–338). Boston: Butterworth-Heinemann.

Armstrong, M.J., & Fitzgerald, M.H. (1996). Culture and disability studies: An anthropological perspective. *Rehabilitation Education, 10,* 247–304.

Ashby, G. (1983a). *A guide to Pohnpei: An island argosy.* Kolonia, Pohnpei: Rainy Day Press.

Ashby, G. (1983b). *Some things of value: Micronesian customs as seen by Micronesians* (2nd ed.). Kolonia, Pohnpei: Rainy Day Press.

Auerbach, S. (1994). Report of Pohnpei Child Health Survey. Findings presented to the Federated States of Micronesia and Pohnpei State Department of Health Services. Pohnpei: Micronesian Seminar.

AvRuskin, T.L. (1988). Neurophysiology and the curative possession trance: The Chinese case. *Medical Anthropology Quarterly, 2* (3), 286–302.

Barnabas, S., & Hezel, F.X. (1993). The changing Pohnpeian family. *Micronesian Counselor,* No. 12. Pohnpei: Micronesian Seminar.

Bourguignon, E. (1976). *Possession.* San Francisco: Chandler & Sharp.

Buckley, T., & Gottlieb, A. (Eds.). (1988). *Blood magic: The anthropology of menstruation*. Berkeley: University of California Press.

Carroll, V. (Ed.). (1970). *Adoption in eastern Oceania*. ASAO Monograph No. 1. Honolulu: University of Hawaii.

Cooksey, N.R. (1995). Pica and olfactory cravings of pregnancy: How deep are the secrets? *Birth, 22* (3), 129–137.

Davis-Floyd, R.E., & Sargent, C.F. (1997). *Childbirth and authoritative knowledge: Cross-cultural perspectives*. Berkeley: University of California Press.

Demory, B.G.H. (1976). *An illusion of surplus: The effect of status rivalry upon family food consumption*. Unpublished Ph.D. diss., University of California at Berkeley.

Dobbin, J.D., & Hezel, F.X. (1996). The distribution of spirit possession and trance in Micronesia. *Pacific Studies, 19* (2), 105–148.

Eisenbruch, M. (1992). Toward a culturally sensitive DSM: Cultural bereavement in Cambodian refugees and the traditional healer as taxonomist. *Journal of Nervous & Mental Disease, 180* (1), 8–10.

Falgout, S. (1993). Tying the knot in Pohnpei. In R.A. Marksbury (Ed.), *The business of marriage: Transformations in Oceanic matrimony* (pp. 127–148). Pittsburgh: University of Pittsburgh.

Fischer, A. (1963). Reproduction in Truk. *Ethnology, 2* (4), 526–540.

Fischer, J.L. (1970). Adoption on Ponape. In V. Carroll (Ed.), *Adoption in eastern Oceania* (pp. 292–313). Honolulu: University of Hawaii Press.

Fitzgerald, M.H. (1983). Possession trance: A healing modality utilizing endogenous healing mechanisms. Unpublished manuscript.

Fitzgerald, M.H. (1984). *A review and critique of the literature on menstrual beliefs*. Unpublished MA Thesis, University of Hawaii, Honolulu.

Fitzgerald, M.H. (1985, May 3–5). *Is menstruation inherently sexual?* Paper presented at the Sixth Conference of the Society for Menstrual Cycle Research. University of Texas Medical Branch, Galveston.

Fitzgerald, M.H. (1989). *Modernization and the menstrual experience among Samoans*. Unpublished Ph.D. diss., University of Hawaii, Honolulu.

Fitzgerald, M.H. (1990). The interplay of culture and symptoms: Menstrual symptoms among Samoans. *Medical Anthropology, 12*, 145–167.

Fitzgerald, M.H. (1992). Is lactation nature's contraceptive? Data from Samoa. *Social Biology, 39* (1–2), 55–64.

Fitzgerald, M.H. (1993). Culture and disability in the Pacific: When does a difference make a difference? *Network Magazine, 3* (2), 7–12.

Fitzgerald, M.H. (1995, 19–20 April). *Cultural breaks in women's knowledge*. Paper presented at the Marcé Pacific Rim Conference: Childbearing and Mental Health—Risk and Remedies (p. 15). Sydney, Australia.

Fitzgerald, M.H. (in collaboration with E. Samuel and L. Phillips). (2000a). *Whisper of the Mother: From Menarche to Menopause among Women in Pohnpei*. Sydney: Author.

Fitzgerald, M.H. (2000b, 15–19 November). *Not much ado about menstruation: Pacific variants on a theme*. Paper presented at the 99th Annual

Meeting of the American Anthropological Association (p. 208). San Francisco.

Fitzgerald, M.H., & Anderson, D.D. (1992). Myth and reality: Providing rehabilitation services in Pacific Island communities. *American Rehabilitation*, Spring, 7–10, 47–48.

Fitzgerald, M.H., & Armstrong, J. (Eds.). (1993). *Culture and disability in the Pacific*. Durham, NH: University of New Hampshire, World Rehabilitation Fund.

Fitzgerald, M.H., & Baker, J. (1993). Rehabilitation services for the Pacific: Meeting the challenge. *Western Journal of Medicine, 159* (1), 50–55.

Fitzgerald, M.H., Ing, V., Ya, T.H., Hay, S.H., Yang, T., Duong, H.L., Barnett, B., Matthey, S., Silove, D., Mitchell, P., & McNamara, J. (1998). *Hear our voices: Trauma, birthing, and mental health among Cambodian women: The Cambodian Women's Project*. Sydney: Transcultural Mental Health Centre.

Fitzgerald, M.H., Yee, H.K.M., Goebert, D.A., & Okamoto, G. (1992). Rehabilitation technicians in rural remote communities. *World Health Forum, 13,* 303–306.

Flear, J., Samo, M., & Hezel, F.X. (1998). *A brief summary of the health priorities seminars conducted in Yap, Chuuk, Kosrae, Pohnpei, and the Marshall Islands*. Kolonia, Pohnpei, FSM: Micronesian Seminar.

Government of the Federated States of Micronesia. (1990). *Digest of Health Statistics 1990*. Pohnpei, FSM: Government of the Federated States of Micronesia, Department of Human Resources Medical and Vital Statistics Office.

Hanlon, D. (1988). *Upon a stone altar: A history of the island of Pohnpei to 1890*. Honolulu: University of Hawaii Press.

Hanna, J.M., & Fitzgerald, M.H. (1993). Acculturation and symptoms: A comparative study of reported health symptoms in three Samoan communities. *Social Science and Medicine, 36* (9), 1169–1180.

Henshaw, S.K. (1999, June). *U.S. teenage pregnancy statistics*. New York: Alan Guttmacher Institute.

Hezel, F.X. (1991). The dilemmas of development: Effects of modernization on three areas of island life. *Micronesian Seminar Occasional Papers*, No. 4. Pohnpei: Micronesian Seminar.

Hezel, F.X. (1993). Culture in crisis: Trends in the Pacific today. *The Micronesian Counselor*, No. 10. Pohnpei: Micronesian Seminar.

Hezel, F.X. (1994a). Culture in crisis: Trends in the Pacific today. *Journal of The Pacific Society, 16* (4), 5–11.

Hezel, F.X. (1994b). Spirit possession in Chuuk: A socio-cultural interpretation. *Journal of The Pacific Society, 17* (1), 1–10.

Hezel, F.X. (1999). *Vitamin A deficiency*. Micronesian Seminar Monthly Discussion Summary, Series 5, No. 1. Pohnpei: Micronesian Seminar.

Jordan, B. (1993). *Birth in four cultures: A crosscultural investigation of childbirth in Yucatan, Holland, Sweden, and the United States* (4th ed.). Prospect Heights, IL: Waveland Press.

Keating, E. (1998a). Honor and stratification in Pohnpei, Micronesia. *American Ethnologist, 25* (3), 399–411.

Keating, E. (1998b). *Power sharing: Language, rank, gender and social space in Pohnpei, Micronesia.* Oxford: Oxford University Press.

Keating, E. (2000). Moments of hierarchy: Constructing social stratification by means of language, food, space, and the body in Pohnpei, Micronesia. *American Anthropologist, 102* (2), 303–320.

Khanna, J. (1999). How women perceive menstruation and their menstrual patterns. *Progress in Human Reproduction Research, 52,* 2–3

Kihleng, K.S. (1996). *Women in exchange: Negotiated relations, practice, and the constitution of female power in processes of cultural reproduction and change in Pohnpei, Micronesia.* Unpublished Ph.D. diss., University of Hawaii, Honolulu.

Kiste, R.C., & Marshall, M. (1999). *American anthropology in Micronesia: An assessment.* Honolulu: University of Hawaii Press.

Lloyd-Puryear, M., Humphrey, J.H., West, K.P., Aniol, K., Mahoney, J., & Keenum, D.G. (1989). Vitamin A deficiency and anemia among Micronesian children. *Nutrition Research, 9,* 1007–1016.

Marcus, M.N. (1991). Child abuse and neglect in Micronesia. *Micronesian Counselor,* No. 2. Pohnpei: Micronesian Seminar.

Marshall, M. (1996). Problematizing impairment: Cultural competence in the Carolines. *Ethnology, 35* (4), 249–263.

Marshall, M. (1999). "Partial connections": Kinship and social organization in Micronesia. In R.C. Kiste & M. Marshall (Eds.), *American anthropology in Micronesia: An assessment* (pp. 107–143). Honolulu: University of Hawaii Press.

Marshall, M., Sexton, R., & Insko, L. (1994). Inhalent abuse in the Pacific Islands: Gasoline sniffing in Chuuk, Federated States of Micronesia. *Pacific Studies, 17* (2), 23–37.

Marshall, M., Sexton, R., & Insko, L. (1996). Gasoline sniffing. *The Micronesian Counselor, 2* (1), 24–33.

National Government Federated States of Micronesia. (1996). *National census report: 1994 FSM Census of population and housing.* Palikir, Pohnpei, FSM: Office of Planning and Statistics, National Government Federated States of Micronesia.

Pacific Basin Maternal and Child Health Resource Center (PBMCH). (1996). *A report of maternal and child health statistics in the U.S.-related Pacific Islands.* Guam: Pacific Basin Maternal and Child Health Resource Center.

Pacific Health Dialog (2000). Auckland, NZ: Resource Books

Petersen, G. (1984). The Ponapean culture of resistance. *Radical History Review, 28–30,* 347–366.

Petersen, G. (1989a). Pohnpei ethnicity and Micronesian nation-building. In M. Howard (Ed.), *Ethnicity and nation building in the Pacific* (pp. 285–308). Tokyo: The United Nations University.

Petersen, G. (1989b). Ponapean chieftainship in the era of the nation-state. In P. Skalnik (Ed.), *Outwitting the state* (pp. 23–39). New Brunswick: Transaction Publishers.

Petersen, G. (1990). Some overlooked complexities in the study of Pohnpei social competency. *Micronesica Suppl, 2,* 137–152.

Petersen, G. (1992). Dancing defiance: The politics of Pohnpeian dance performances. *Pacific Studies, 15* (4), 13–28.

Petersen, G. (1993). Kanengamah and Pohnpei's politics of concealment. *American Anthropologist, 95* (2), 334–352.

Petersen, G. (1995). The complexity of power, the subtlety of kava. *Canberra Anthropology, 18* (1 & 2), 34–60.

Pinsker, E.C. (1997). *Point of order, point of change: Nation, culture and community in the Federated States of Micronesia.* Unpublished Ph.D. diss., University of Chicago.

Pohnpei State Government. (1996). *Pohnpei state census report: 1994 FSM Census of Population and Housing.* Kolonia, Pohnpei FSM: Office of the Governor, Statistics Section, Pohnpei State Government.

Pretrick, E. (1997). Family planning in the Federated States of Micronesia: Past and present. *Pacific Health Dialog, 4* (1), 111–112.

Ram, K., & Jolly, M. (Eds.). (1998). *Maternities and modernities.* Cambridge, England: Cambridge University Press.

Rose, E.A., Porcerelli, J.H., & Neale, A.V. (2000). Pica: Common but commonly missed. *Journal of the American Board of Family Practitioners, 13* (5), 353–358.

Rubinstein, D. (1994). Changes in the Micronesian family structure leading to alcoholism, suicide, and child abuse and neglect. *Micronesian Counselor,* No. 15. Pohnpei: Micronesian Seminar.

Savetta, R.B. (1986). Pica: An overview. *American Family Physician, 33* (5), 181–185.

Schneider, D. (1968). Abortion and depopulation on a Pacific island. In A. Vayda (Ed.), *People and cultures of the Pacific* (pp. 383–406). New York: Natural History Press.

Singer, M., Arnold, C., Fitzgerald, M., Madden, L., & Voight von Legat, C. (1984). Hypoglycemia: A controversial illness in U.S. society. *Medical Anthropology, 8* (1), 1–35.

Singer, M., Fitzgerald, M.H., Madden, L., Voight von Legat, C., & Arnold, C.D. (1987). The sufferer's experience of hypoglycemia. In J.A. Roth & P. Conrad (Eds.), *The experience and management of chronic illness (Research in the sociology of health care)* Vol. 6, pp. 147–175. Greenwich, CT: JAI Press.

Snowden, R., & Christian, B. (1983). *Patterns and perceptions of menstruation: A World Health Organization international collaborative study in Egypt, Pakistan, Philippines, Republic of Korea, United Kingdom and Yugoslavia.* New York: St. Martin's Press.

South Pacific Commission. (1994). *Pacific Island populations*: Report prepared by the South Pacific Commission for the International Conference on Population and Development, 5–13 September 1994, Cairo. Noumea, New Caledonia: South Pacific Commission.

Sowell, A., Gonzaga, P.S., Englberger, L., Schendel, D., Elymore, J., & Huff, D. (2000). *Vitamin A deficiency and anemia among preschool children and their mothers or female caregivers in Yap and Kosrae States, Federated States of Micronesia.* Paper presented at XX IVACG Meeting.

Turner, V. (1967). *Forest of symbols.* Ithaca: Cornell University Press.

Ward, M.C. (1989). *Nest in the wind: Adventures in anthropology on a tropical island.* Prospect Heights, IL: Waveland Press.

Ward, R.L. (1977). *Curing on Ponape: A medical ethnography.* Unpublished Ph.D. diss., Tulane University, New Orleans.

Walker, S.B. (1972). *Ceremonial spirit possession in Africa and Afro-America.* Netherlands: E.J. Brill.

Yasuo, H. (1940). The customs and manners of child-birth among the south sea islanders. *Japanese Journal of Ethnology*, 6 (3), 36–46.

Author Index

Subject Index

U.W.E.L. LEARNING RESOURCES

About the Author

MAUREEN H. FITZGERALD is Senior Lecturer, School of Occupation and Leisure Sciences, the University of Sydney.